OLD HOUSES IN HOLLAND

TEXT AND ILLUSTRATIONS BY SYDNEY R. JONES, WITH SOME ADDITIONAL PLATES IN COLOUR AFTER OTHER ARTISTS

STUDIO EDITIONS
LONDON

First published by 'The Studio' Ltd. London in 1912.

This edition published 1986 by Studio Editions,
a division of Bestseller Publications Ltd,
Princess House, 50 Eastcastle Street, London W1N 7AP.

ISBN 1 85170 050 1

Printed and bound in Yugoslavia by Grafoimpex.

PREFATORY NOTE

THE Editor desires to express his indebtedness to the following, who have rendered valuable assistance in the preparation of this volume: Mr. A. Pit, Director of the Nederlandsch Museum voor Geschiedenis en Kunst, and other officials of the Rijks Museum, Amsterdam; Messrs. P. C. J. A. Boeles and D. Draaisma, of the Friesch Museum, Leeuwarden; Dr. B. van Rijswijk, Secretary of the Vereeniging Oud-Dordrecht; Mr. W. Polman Kruseman, Secretary of the Zeeuwsch Genootschap der Wetenschappen, Middelburg; and the Directors of the British Museum, the Victoria and Albert Museum, the National Gallery, and the Wallace Collection, London.

ILLUSTRATIONS IN COLOUR

CONTENTS.

INTRODUCTION

INTRODUCTION

IT is in the old towns of Holland that the architectural expression of the Dutch people is to be sought. Theirs was an intimate and human architecture, concerned with everyday events, and it developed out of the civil and domestic life. Many of the towns continue to be busy and prosperous, and new buildings here and there crowd in upon the picturesque groups of houses that for centuries have clustered round the great churches and market-places: in others, the active days of commerce are over, the merchants come no more, and the streets and waterways are quiet. But all Dutch towns having any pretension to age possess, to a wonderful degree, what may be termed an old-world atmosphere. Much of their charm, it is true, is due to the rivers and canals that encircle and intersect them in all directions, imparting a sense of quaintness and novelty; but it is the extraordinary number of old buildings still existing, unchanged in form since the days when they were erected and mellowed by ages of sun and rain, that ever appeal to the eye and imagination. The fantastic gables and red roofs, above which rise slender spires and belfries surmounted by leaden flèches and wrought vanes, together with the waterways and canal life, the windmills, and changing skies, are as characteristic now as when the masters of the great Dutch School of painting were living and working. Such scenes were to them inspiration; to picture the intimate events associated was their delight. If the painters have gone—and with them the arquebusiers and governors and burgomasters—the gables, the sunlit courts, and many other familiar features remain.

The peculiar geographical conditions that have always existed in Holland have affected in no small degree the development of the land and the temperament of the people. Most of the country is below sea level. Behind the dunes and dykes the sea threatens inundation; the fear of accident by flood has kept the nation watchful and in perpetual war with its ancient enemy. The influence of this natural check has been far-reaching. It has produced the system of canals, determined the character of the landscape, made accordant life and work, method, regularity and order, and brought philosophy and fortitude to the national mind. In the domain of building, as in other spheres, water has been a powerful underlying agent affecting the evolution of style, just as the mountains, forests and deserts of other countries have imparted distinction to architecture.

Side by side with the external conditions imposed by Nature, conditions that, if accepted, might well be expected to have produced an attitude of extreme lack of initiative in those living amongst them, the Dutch have ever been an enterprising people. The same spirit that defied and conquered the inroads of the sea characterised their dealings in the domain of commerce. Trade was to them the great business of life. From very early times, and continuing for a long period, the prosperity of the Low

Countries was foremost in Europe. The towns became centres of busy and pulsative life, the homes of virile civil and domestic communities. Many old buildings still existing, town halls, weigh houses, trade and guild halls, warehouses and merchants' premises, bear witness to those strenuous days. An architecture in close touch with the events of the times developed through, and by reason of the successes achieved by industry and sustained advances of conquest and colonization.

The phase of domestic art which is reviewed in this volume was essentially the expression of a nation urgently concerned with the material, matter-of-fact side of everyday life, and bore close kindred to its needs, its aspirations and its achievements; it was corporeal rather than spiritual in aspect, reflective of the market-place, the fireside and the home. And while the continuous building tradition of certain other countries was allied to ecclesiasticism, or was a movement instigated by the aristocracy, in Holland it was democratic in general trend, an art bound up in the interests of the people and existing for their good and welfare. It was urban rather than rural in its principles. Unlike the English growth, where the native building art developed vigorously and lingered longest in the countryside—as many an old village, manor-house or farm will demonstrate—the equivalent vernacular Dutch development was pre-eminently of the towns, and trade was the influence that gave it life. In a country notable for its manufactures and commercial activities men congregated together for mutual gain. A sturdy race they were, unimpressionable, but kindly and charitable, and their comfortable homes were in keeping with their temperament.

To better appreciate the course of architectural development, it will be well to briefly cite the main circumstances connected with these towns and with the country's history. Records of Dutch towns prior to the twelfth century are scanty, although at that time orderly government had begun to develop. Then followed the municipal charters, many dating from the thirteenth century. These charters were granted by the feudal lords to the townspeople and secured to them certain rights and protection in return for taxation and levies; justice was administered by various governing bodies and magistrates, and the municipal finances were properly supervised. There thus grew up a strong communal movement which was steadily developed and strengthened. Then it was that the cities began their era of great prosperity and each became practically self-governing and semi-independent. Revenue was derived from the river commerce and markets, over-sea trading, and from the industries which were fostered. So powerful did they become, so energetic was their municipal life, so well organised their trade, that these cities came to be reckoned, together with the neighbouring towns of Flanders, the most prosperous and wealthy in the world. As time went on the chief cities became members of the Hanseatic League, which influential association embraced trading colonies in places as far apart as London, Visby on the island of Gotland, Novgorod the Great in Russia, Hamburg, Amsterdam and Kampen on the Zuider Zee. Through the impetus of this remarkable movement, the long-continued

BREDA, NORTH BRABANT

5

commercial relations between England and Holland were established. About the middle of the thirteenth century Hanse merchants settled in London, obtained privileges from Henry III., founded the Steelyard, and there developed a flourishing trade. The intercourse between the two countries was very considerable, and it was of the utmost importance to the Netherlands that nothing should happen to weaken their good relations with England. For England was then the principal wool-producing country of Europe, the only place, in fact, able to supply it in large quantities, and the men of the Low Countries, famed above all for their skill as weavers and depending upon the woollen industry for their greatest wealth, were eager buyers of English wool in the raw state. In the fifteenth century, through dissension and war, the cities of Holland were ejected from the Hanseatic League; but the Dutch, with their fine ships and business acumen, continued to prosper and carried their conquests by trade into far-distant lands.

It was while at the height of their material success that the provinces of Holland came under the dominion of the house of Burgundy. The peculiar independent constitution of the cities promoted rivalry between them, rather than a common national interest which would have been best for the preservation of their just rights. They were heavily taxed and oppressed and were continually at variance with the ruling power, fighting for the redress of their grievances. By the first half of the sixteenth century the kingdom of the Netherlands had passed to the Emperor Charles V., King of Spain, and Philip, his son, inherited his father's throne. He thereby became monarch of vast territories. Philip determined to utterly subjugate the provinces and carried out a policy of relentless persecution. The people rebelled, brutal punishment followed, and they became victims of the worst excesses of the Inquisition. Deeds of cruelty, tyranny and murder, almost unparalleled in history, were enacted. In those dark days arose that great champion of the people, "William the Silent," Prince of Orange, the "father of his fatherland." Intent on defending the liberties of the nation, he gathered around him a company of gallant spirits, and, principally at his own expense, commenced what at first appeared to be a hopeless struggle. But early victories, hardly won, roused a cowed populace to action. The nation embarked upon the memorable Eighty Years' War, which resulted in the Spanish yoke being overthrown and the founding of the Dutch Republic. William was basely assassinated at Delft in 1584, and Maurice, his second son, succeeded him as *Stadtholder.* He was ambitious, shrewd, and skilled in the arts of war, and under his rule, and that of his brother Frederick Henry, who succeeded him in 1625, the fortunes of the Dutch gradually rose high. Through times of trial and suffering, hardships endured and conquests won, they emerged valorous and strong, a nation of heroes. Triumphs of arms by land and sea, successes of the merchant fleets and navigators who explored remote parts of the world, the founding of colonies, and ingenuity on the part of the workers in home manufactures, characterised a notable period of great prosperity; the Dutch became supreme in trade, chief rulers of the sea, and accumulated vast wealth. As the seventeenth century advanced commercial welfare

MONNIKENDAM, NORTH HOLLAND

continued to increase. Admirals Tromp and De Ruyter swept the seas, gaining brilliant naval victories; in 1667 the safety of London itself was threatened by the appearance of the Dutch fleet in the Thames. But the mastery of the sea eventually passed to England and from that time the fortunes of the Dutch declined. The election of William III.—who had married Princess Mary, daughter of the Duke of York—to the English throne in 1689 marked the close of Holland's greatest days.

Early Dutch secular architecture is in the spirit of the late Gothic style. The most valuable monuments of that period are the civic buildings which herald a time when public life—as opposed to ecclesiastical—assumed an importance and dignity capable of being symbolized in brick and stone; when power acquired by trade found expression in its own distinctive forms, and the wealthy burghers of the towns erected municipal buildings which stand for all time as the embodiment of their ideals. Such is the Town Hall at Middelburg by Ant. Keldermans the Younger, one of that famous family of architects of Malines. It is a stone erection of fine proportions, enriched with a wealth of detail, sculptured figures, sunk panelling and many turrets; tiers of dormers break up the roof surface and the whole is surmounted by a noble and boldly conceived tower. At Veere, not far distant, is a smaller example (opposite) built in 1474 by another member of the Keldermans family. While owning some similarity to its fellow at Middelburg, the treatment is simpler, but the proportions are exquisite, and the peculiar grace of the belfry is outstanding. The characteristic richness of surface decoration which was then common may also be seen on the sandstone façade of the "Gemeenlandshuis" at Delft, with its elaborate traceries and parapet belonging to the early sixteenth century. The aforementioned are stone buildings and betray the influence of French Gothic, but the especially individual Netherlandish interpretation of Gothic was developed in the brick architecture. Brickwork was much employed and the nature of the material—not so responsive as stone in the hands of the craftsmen—limited the possibilities of ornamental treatment. Detail had to be simplified and adapted to the means available for carrying it out; the example from Nijmegen (p. 11), dated 1544, furnishes an instance of how it was handled. It is in this early brickwork that the germs of the Dutch transitional Renaissance style are to be traced; its root principles were derived not only from the public buildings, but from the churches also—vast piles whose bold masses and ornaments were logically developed out of the material, and whose millions of little bricks, jointed together, stand as impressive memorials of patient labour.

Mediæval domestic work followed in the wake of the civic. Not many examples remain. Of those that have survived most belong to the late fifteenth or the first half of the sixteenth century. The current forms of the period were employed—panelling and projecting surface decoration, more often in brickwork than stone; arched window-heads ornamented with tracery; circular brick turrets surmounted by conical roofs; stepped gables having pinnacles rising from the copings; steep roofs pierced by dormers; and the somewhat florid, rich, but carefully wrought detail.

"INTERIOR OF A DUTCH HOUSE." FROM AN OIL PAINTING BY PIETER DE HOOCH.

(In the National Gallery, London.)

(In the Wallace Collection, London.)

"INTERIOR WITH WOMAN PEELING APPLES."
FROM AN OIL PAINTING BY PIETER DE HOOCH.

VEERE, ZEELAND

9

In contrast to the scarcity of Gothic domestic buildings, those of the Transitional period—from Gothic to Renaissance—are very numerous. Many examples are to be found in the old towns where rows of houses, much out of the perpendicular, rise from the canalsides and paved roadways. They are narrow and very high and are surmounted by gables which are often of fantastic shape and curious outline, picturesque from the draughtsman's point of view and full of subject for the painter. Strange though it now seems, and quite beyond reasonable explanation, the greatest art movement that Holland has ever known flourished at the close of those troublous times when she was at war with Spain. It was then that the painters, with startling suddenness, came into their full powers, and Hals, Rembrandt, Van der Helst, Gerard Dou, Paul Potter, Jan Steen, Ruysdael and De Hooch, with a host of brilliant companions, followed in quick succession. They created a new art, a school of painting with original conceptive views and unrivalled executive skill. Contemporaneously with this artistic activity developed the peculiarly specific Dutch style of domestic architecture. Existing examples prove how energetically the building craft was then carried on, and show how its characteristics were matured during the closing years of the sixteenth century and onwards through the century following. Many of the Town Halls and Weigh Houses, which set the fashion for the private dwellings, are of this time; Leiden 1598, Haarlem 1602, Nijmegen 1612, Bolsward 1614, Workum 1650, and numerous others.

It was in the sixteenth century that the influence of the Renaissance gained ground in Holland, and with it came new canons and new impulses, revived interest in classical literature and art. And in connection with it, it is significant to note that Erasmus, one of the most distinguished of the Humanists, was born at Rotterdam in 1466; during a life of much travel and varied residence he was often in the Low Countries, prosecuting his own self-culture and advocating his doctrines.

The Transitional period lasted long and the buildings associated with it in many ways resemble those of England, erected in the style known as Elizabethan. The real significance of the revolutionary Renaissance art was not grasped or understood. The Gothic form of house long held its own and to it was added the heavy Dutch interpretation of the newer style, a rendering showing French rather than Italian feeling. But nevertheless, however well or ill applied, the use of Classic motifs in architecture became a firmly-established and general practice.

But the great changes in religious and intellectual thought that transpired during the sixteenth century did not so quickly influence the domain of architecture as might be supposed. No sudden breach with the inherited style occurred, although the ancient life and faith were passing. The Gothic tradition, which had been handed down from generation to generation, continued on. The national temperament was opposed to innovation, and the Dutch people clung to that which had been evolved through long years of experiment; they were unwilling to give up those forms that had been satisfying to their forefathers. So the new

NIJMEGEN, GELDERLAND (DATED 1544)

fashion in architecture was at first but tardily accepted and made little headway against the olden practices. Early tentative efforts were confined to novelties of detail introduced in gable ornaments, window-heads and doorways ; the traditional forms of building remained unaltered, and fresh types of ornament were simply added to them for no very definite or intelligent reason. As time went on the Renaissance influence gradually became more established, but there was evidently no unanimity of opinion on the merits of it. Some looked upon it with favour ; others viewed it with suspicion and preferred to keep to that which had served so well for preceding generations. As a consequence, the development was not uniform throughout the country. Thus a house at Alkmaar, bearing the late date of 1673, has arched window-heads and step gable terminated with a pointed arch quite in the Gothic manner ; while a façade erected at Zwolle one hundred and two years earlier unmistakably betrays its Classic origin by the details with which it is adorned.

After a changeful period, during which the architectural impulses were halting between the acceptance of the new and the retention of the old, men who directed public taste eventually adopted what they understood to be the Renaissance ideas. Behind them was a strong tide of inherited tradition which continued to flow on. To it they brought their own interpretation of the new movement, and the two forces ran side by side for many years.

Foremost among the earlier architects who turned to classicism for fresh inspiration were Lieven de Key, Hendrik de Keyzer and Cornelius Danckerts. Hendrik de Keyzer was born at Utrecht in 1565 and died at Amsterdam in 1621. He was appointed architect to the city of Amsterdam in 1594, and his name is connected with buildings both in that town and elsewhere. One of his most notable works is the monument erected at Delft to the memory of William the Silent. Cornelius Danckerts was associated with de Keyzer and lived from 1561 to 1631. Born at Ghent about the year 1560, Lieven de Key worked principally at Haarlem and Leiden. He was the author of the celebrated Meat Market at Haarlem, a remarkable building which has evoked both praise and disparagement ; it was completed in 1603. He was responsible for the design of other civic buildings as well as numerous private dwellings. Such men as these had their followers and founded schools of architecture in the places of their professional activities. There was thus a vigorous body of men working at Haarlem ; while Amsterdam, which had become virtually the political and commercial capital as well as the centre of the arts, had its own assembly of architects who were particularly energetic in the city and exercised great influence in the adjacent districts. The results of their accomplishments are still apparent, and the many large and sober gabled houses suggest to the imagination the comparative splendour of seventeenth-century Amsterdam.

The buildings of this period are quaint and charming. If somewhat lacking in serious architectonic qualities, they are inseparably connected with the national sentiments ; they stand as lasting evidences of human

DORDRECHT, SOUTH HOLLAND

emotion expressed through the medium of brick and stone. The streets lined with ancient houses are witnesses of a great past, and bring to remembrance those strong and earnest men who honoured hearth and threshold and fought to save their fatherland from tyranny and threatened ruin. Above all, the structures bear upon them the impress of the intellectual life which was concerned with their production. The work itself is thoroughly Dutch in character, full of suggestion, and the materials are well handled. That of the early Renaissance is the best, and in it the two streams of thought—mediæval and classic—are seen harmoniously blended. A good example from Leiden, by Lieven de Key, is illustrated opposite; signs of the new influence are obvious in the details, yet it has the traditional form of stepped gable; while there is a freedom of handling discernible in the disposition of the ground floor features which was dictated by convenience rather than symmetrical arrangement. All the work, however, was not so reasonable as this. Gables of extraordinary and curious outline began to appear, remarkable certainly for fertility of invention, but often lacking in delicacy and restraint. Isolated stone ornaments, unconnected with constructive principles, were applied to vacant wall spaces. They were decorated with lion-heads, armorial bearings, strapwork, cartouches, winged heads and panels in relief, all vigorously carved. Many of the subjects were seemingly derived from published pattern books and decorative designs, and lack that independence of conception which distinguishes all inspired craftsmanship.

Evidence goes to prove that the men who made the designs for the buildings had not yet become detached from the building trades. They were not architects within the present meaning of that term. They were described as masons, stonecutters, and the like, and no doubt were master-builders who, in addition to supplying the design, had a personal hand in the execution of the work of their own particular craft. The idea that a trained director should conceive the work as a whole, and marshal all the supplementary arts to proper subjugation, had not yet been evolved. Architecture as a separate force was not recognised.

Results automatically grew out of the united efforts of the sculptors, bricklayers, carpenters and masons who were engaged on the same production. So de Key, in addition to acting as a designer, was the city mason of Haarlem; H. de Keyzer was sculptor to the city of Amsterdam; and these are typical instances of the conditions then prevailing. It is also not surprising to find in this country, where government by municipalities was so well developed, that the architects were often official servants of the towns. Two such are mentioned above; Dryfhout was town architect of Middelburg, and Ambrosius van Hanenberch held a similar position at 's Hertogenbosch.* The demand for qualified men to protect and guide the public artistic needs was appreciated, a wise and excellent practice from which present-day authorities in England might well take a lesson.

With the advancing seventeenth century came a keener desire for the employment of purer forms of Renaissance art. Architects turned their

* "Biographical Sketches of Dutch Architects."—MSS. by J. B. Weenink.

LEIDEN, RHIJNLAND (DATED 1612)

thoughts to the Italian ideal, which they modified, yet preserved in its essential characteristics. Chief among the exponents of the developed style were Jacob van Campen and Phillippus Vinckboons, both of Amsterdam; and Pieter Post of Haarlem. The massive Town Hall of Amsterdam—now the Royal Palace—by van Campen, is one of the most important buildings of this period. It was erected between the years 1648 and 1655. But the severe classic ideas, directing towards uniformity and symmetrical arrangements, were never really at home, nor did they displace the weakening influence of inherited tradition. In the general mass of work the Dutch national genius continued to assert itself. Up to the time when the native architecture became devoid of character and personality, the houses and trade buildings in which the people lived and worked—even if of strange appearance or sometimes fantastic beyond description—retained an unmistakable flavour of the vernacular and owned something of that playfulness and quaint invention that were the heritage of mediæval times.

It is fitting to conclude this Introduction by referring to the effect of Dutch upon English architecture. For our style of domestic building has in the past owed something to knowledge gained from the Low Countries; details have been derived from the Dutch and their practices adopted. Most obviously the influence is to be seen in the Eastern counties, although it penetrated more or less throughout the country; Staffordshire can show it as well as Norfolk, Wiltshire as well as Kent. To those men of the Netherlands who early engaged in English commerce the germs of this influence are to be traced. Not that many of these foreigners were actively connected with the building trades, but, during a long period of trading intercourse and settlement by merchants and artisans, they, as a matter of course, left distinct impressions of their own ideas. Onward from the fourteenth century the influx of Flemings and Dutchmen into England was considerable and the reasons for their coming various. Apart from the traders, skilled artisans were encouraged to settle for the purpose of improving the home manufactures. Oppression, too, was responsible for many immigrants; to cite an instance, thousands of people left Holland when the harsh Duke of Alva, acting for Philip of Spain, was in 1567 appointed commander of the forces, and numbers of them found refuge in England. But the presence of foreigners such as these, most of whom were not engaged in the building crafts, had only an indirect effect upon the local architecture. It was the imported artificers, coming from Germany as well as the Netherlands, who brought a new development to English building. "Throughout the reign of Elizabeth," writes Professor Blomfield, "their influence was in the air and predominant." The results of it are obvious in work then erected, notably in the long series of country houses with strapwork ornament, peculiar decoration of porches and fireplaces, and much patterned woodwork. Again, with the advent of Dutch William to the English throne, further new features were introduced and they are especially traceable in the admirable brickwork of the Queen Anne style. But the lasting and altogether good effect of Dutch

HAARLEM, NORTH HOLLAND

influence was on traditional, rather than academic architecture, on those quiet and unpretentious buildings of the countryside. Here the foreign motives were almost imperceptibly blended with those existing, neither suddenly nor inharmoniously. A feature was added here, a detail there, yet the work remained truly English in character. Old villages can yet show buildings that bear upon them traces of an alien hand, or embody ideas drawn from other than local sources of inspiration. Such are the East Kentish cottages at Sandwich, Ickham, Reading Street and Sarre; the halls and manor-houses of Norfolk, Suffolk, and Essex, with corbie-stepped and curved gables; the high brick barns of the Eastern counties; and endless picturesque groupings of certain distinction that exist up and down the land. The industrious settlers from over the water certainly brought something to our traditional architecture, gave it qualities that helped to make it what it was. And when they came to erect their dwellings on foreign soil, they cherished the memory of their own country, and turned their thoughts to home and to the houses on the tree-lined streets and waterways of Holland.

BRIGDAMME, ZEELAND

DIVISION I

THE DEVELOPMENT OF DOMESTIC ARCHITECTURE

I.—THE DEVELOPMENT OF DOMESTIC ARCHITECTURE.

THE only really abundant building materials in Holland were bricks. Stone was available in limited quantities, but not readily so. Brick-earths there were in plenty, and brick-building has been practised continuously from the dawn of Dutch architecture to the present day. The inhabitants, after long and intimate association, became very proficient in the use of bricks, skilful in applying them, and apt to quickly realize the possibilities afforded by this material. There is, therefore, a great deal of old work of exceptional interest which is, in addition, valuable for the suggestions it presents.

The creation and development of an architectural style, depending upon brickwork as the medium for its execution, call into being considerable powers of ingenuity. For the limitations of bricks are definite and circumscribed ; the unit is small and its size not subject to variation. Moreover, enrichment can only be obtained by careful disposition and arrangement of the units, and the almost unlimited scope possessed by stone, wood or plaster—both in respect to size of parts and effects of surface decoration—is nearly non-existent. Difficulties such as these have to be realised and overcome, but good results are not easily secured. The preconceived ideas in the mind, the general proportions, and the disposition of features, are governed to a degree by the nature of the building material. And for these reasons. The bonding of the walling, colour arrangements, width and finish of the mortar joints, and the precise manner of forming details, all contribute markedly to the ultimate appearance of the whole. Good brickwork depends, even more than other forms of building, upon a complete understanding of the

GRONINGEN (1509)

BOXMEER, NORTH BRABANT

capabilities of the medium ; skill in manipulating it is secondary only to capacity for design.

It was in the use of bricks that the Dutch were especially successful. Qualified by experience gained through years of experiment, their achievements were dexterous and often daring. They were thoroughly at home with brickwork, alive to its restrictions as well as its possibilities, and they handled it in a spontaneous and reasonable way. All the features and details of some buildings had to be suitably designed for execution in this not very pliable material—gables (page 21), windows, doorways (shown above), decoration, mouldings and traceries. Problems such as these, definitely existing, were satisfactorily solved. The craftsmen thought in brickwork, as it were, and forms were more or less dictated by the means available for carrying them out. Not that stone was ignored ; on the contrary, it was doubtless used when it could be obtained, as our illustrations plainly show. Thus, it was employed not only for ornamental details but often for the entire structures. Wood had its uses too, as may be seen in the half-timbered houses at Dordrecht or the wooden-fronted ones at Gorinchem (Gorcum), illustrated opposite ; and plaster entered into the construction of many country buildings. But the prevailing conditions brought about an advanced development of brickwork and through it the vital building tradition was evolved.

The old bricks themselves were particularly well shaped and the proportion of height to length gave a long and narrow appearance. How narrow

GORINCHEM (GORCUM), SOUTH HOLLAND

BREDA, NORTH BRABANT

24

(*In the Ryks Museum, Amsterdam.*)

"DUTCH INTERIOR." FROM AN OIL PAINTING BY PIETER DE HOOCH.

(In the Ryks Museum, Amsterdam.)

"THE LETTER." FROM AN OIL PAINTING BY JOHANNES VERMEER.

MIDDELBURG, ZEELAND

they actually were will be realised when it is stated that it not infrequently happens we find them no more than 1¼ inches high. Some of the sizes noted are 1¼ inches by 6¾ inches to 7 inches at Workum; 1½ inches by 7 inches at Breda (page 24); 1½ inches by 8½ inches, and 1¾ inches by 7 inches to 8½ inches at Haarlem; and 2 inches by 9 inches at 's Hertogenbosch. They were laid with five, six, or seven courses to the foot, and sometimes the door and window openings were formed with smaller sized bricks than those used for the main walling. It was only rarely that comparatively large bricks were employed. Some may be seen in the walls of the old Abbey at Middelburg, and "Thvis van Leeninge" (page 25), situated in the same town, has bricks measuring 2½ inches by 9½ inches; while a building at Franeker, in Friesland, is carried out in unusually large bricks, which vary in size from 3 inches to 3½ inches by 10½ inches to 11½ inches. The joints are widest in the older work and were either finished with dark mortar, no lighter in tone than the bricks, or were raked out and pointed up with light mortar. The bond almost universally adopted was that known by the name of "English" and not, as is often erroneously stated, "Flemish." English bond consists of alternate courses of headers and stretchers; that is to say, one course of bricks, all placed longways, upon a course all laid endways, and so continuously up the wall. Flemish bond, rarely to be seen in Holland, has alternate headers and stretchers in every course. Dutch brickwork shows a wide range of colouring. Some is very dark and of a purple tint; some is yellow, particularly in the neighbourhood of Dordrecht; red bricks there are in every town; while at Breda they gradate from lemon yellow to a delicate salmon pink. It will be perceived that materials such as these offered means for harmonious combinations. The possibilities were appreciated, and about the country there exist many happy effects which were secured by blending the various coloured bricks. It was a favourite method to build walls with parti-coloured bands running horizontally through them in the manner shown

FRANEKER, FRIESLAND

DORDRECHT, SOUTH HOLLAND

from Franeker (page 26), where four courses of red bricks interchange with one of yellow. Mouldings and surrounds to openings often contrasted with the prevailing colour of the building. As an illustration of this, the example from Dordrecht (below) may be cited ; the walls are formed with yellow bricks and the decorated window-heads with red. In addition to effects obtained by colour harmonies, enrichment was secured by applying moulded and shaped brickwork. It was confined principally to the doorways, windows and string courses, and how successful this system of ornamentation can be will be realised by further reference to the two above-mentioned drawings. Among other familiar features of Dutch buildings are the mosaic decorations which generally occupy the arched spaces over window-heads. Made up of simple units—square or shaped bricks and little pieces of stone—they were set together to form repeating patterns and devices. Many of the houses, such as that at Dordrecht (page 27), attain distinction by reason of these interesting and freely rendered details, and they will be more fully considered in the following chapter on exterior features.

Pantiles were almost universally used for roof-coverings in the towns, while in the country thatching was freely employed. Under certain conditions the good qualities of pantiles show conspicuously. Where the country is level and the landscape low, and big changing sky-effects constantly recur, they look particularly homely and suitable. Their curved surfaces quickly respond to play of light, becoming successively bright in the sunlight or mellow-toned in the shadow. They have the appearance, too, of being well able to withstand the wind and the rain. Holland is a country having the attributes for the successful use of these tiles ; moreover, they blended in every way with the prevailing brick architecture, both of the towns and of the villages, as is shown by the illustrations from Haarlem (page 29) and St. Laurens (page 31). They were not always of that bright red colour usually associated with pantiles. Many were made from a grey clay and look not unpleasing ; especially in the town and neighbourhood of Zutphen they can be well

DORDRECHT (DATED 1702)

HAARLEM, NORTH HOLLAND

SPAARWOUDE, NORTH HOLLAND

ST. LAURENS, NEAR MIDDELBURG, ZEELAND

observed. The thatched roofs of the countryside do not present any special characteristics. They were contrived to accomplish their purpose in a straightforward way. Brought down directly from ridge to eaves, or arranged pyramidally, they have no added decoration in straw-work. The ridge was protected by a course of half-round tiles of which the farmhouse at Spaarwoude (page 30) furnishes an example, and the roof of this building, arranged part in thatch and part in pantiles, is an instance of a fairly prevalent practice.

Passing from the consideration of building materials to that of planning, it may be stated as a general rule that the ground plans of the old work were usually determined by the exigencies of practical requirements. The very narrow frontage of many of the houses gave little latitude for variation of interior disposition : for it will be noticed that the majority of the houses were built with gable-ends facing to the streets, and these consequently became the principal elevations. The measurement from front to back of each was thus much greater than that from side to side. The economical and practical way of treating such an area would be to arrange a passage at the side, directly through from front to back, which would, as well, give access to the rooms and stairs ; and this is what was generally done. Such a passage, sketched from the outside pavement, is shown on this page. This expedient was not necessary when the building had a wider frontage, and in such a case the way through was often placed more or less centrally, in the manner illustrated from Alkmaar on page 33. On the other hand, the narrow house at Hoorn (page 34) has a central entrance, and here it gives immediate access to the front room. But the passage was an important feature of Dutch planning and gave the fundamental idea for general disposition.

HAARLEM, NORTH HOLLAND

The internal arrangements were disclosed by the elevations and a guiding principle of Gothic design was thereby followed. The positions of

ALKMAAR, NORTH HOLLAND (DATED 1609)

HOORN, NORTH HOLLAND (DATED 1612)

MIDDELBURG, ZEELAND

HOORN, NORTH HOLLAND

lofty rooms, ways of access, staircases and different floor levels, were as much as possible made obvious on the outside of the buildings. This practice led to many happy results. Not fettered by artificial conventions or limited by unyielding laws, the designers were able to give scope to their invention. Utility and convenience set the theme for spontaneous fancy to adorn. These were the motive powers, the guiding impulses that lay behind the early work, and they continued to operate with more or less force for many generations. The series of houses in the "Balans" at Middelburg (page 35) furnishes a good example of a group that owed its inception to such influences. While there is harmony between part and part no two are alike. One house is higher than its fellow ; one comes forward over the paved way while another recedes. Doorways and windows are conveniently, but not too evenly disposed. The brightly painted window-shutters give lively colour, and isolated features—such as the staircase turret seen on the right—show with telling effect. Gables of differing shape break the skyline.

HOORN, NORTH HOLLAND

37

Utilitarian in lighting the rooms of the roofs, the dormers æsthetically serve to carry the eye up to the ridges. The whole impression, if irregular, is picturesque to a degree. Contemplating an effect such as this, so powerful in its human appeal to the eye and mind, it is difficult to appreciate those arguments which are advanced against principles capable of giving such satisfying results.

The most characteristic essential of domestic architecture in Holland is the steeply-pitched gable. It was derived from Gothic sources. Gables owning this influence almost invariably have the lines of their two ascending sides broken by a series of steps which continue upwards from base to apex. They are consequently called "stepped," and such gables will be observed in the drawing from Middelburg mentioned above. The acute rake of the gables determined the slant of the roofs. This circumstance, together with the fact that houses usually had little frontage to the streets, gave great roof spaces incapable of being adequately lighted by windows inserted in the walls. So the fore part consisted of a room (or rooms) which was generally assigned to servants, and the rear area, lighted by dormers, was used for storing and kindred purposes, one all-important among the latter being that of "drying washing." These dormers were quite important factors in architectural composition ; each had hinged and painted shutters and a little steep roof. Sometimes they were elaborated, as may be seen, for instance, in the drawing from Hoorn (page 37). The dormer eventually became a much developed feature. In examples such as those shown from Leiden (page 39), where two of the houses are not ended by a gable, the main roof would be hipped back. A certain number of dwellings were built with one of the longest sides occupying the main frontage. The house at

WOUDRICHEM, NORTH BRABANT

LEIDEN, RHIJNLAND

MIDDELBURG, ZEELAND

40

NIJMEGEN, GELDERLAND (DATED 1606)

ZUTPHEN, GELDERLAND (see opposite page)

Hoorn (page 36) was so constructed. The floor-joists, carried through the walling, are exposed to view; they project beyond the face of the ground floor wall and support an overhanging upper storey. Similar examples occur at Vlissingen (Flushing), and there the joist-ends are carved with representations of small human heads, each of different design.

Very noticeable, both in early and later work, is the great height of ground-floor rooms and passages. They not uncommonly measure from eleven to thirteen feet, or even more, from floor to ceiling. The windows, proportionate to the rooms, are extremely lofty. Over entrance doorways are fanlights of conspicuous size, which are occasionally nearly as large as the doors themselves. Some houses, with very high front rooms abutting on the street, have at the back two stories contained within this same height. The example from Woudrichem (page 38) is disposed in this way; the fore part of the hall, from which the drawing was made, together with the adjoining room are almost twice as lofty as the passage seen beyond; the stairs give access to the imposed intermediate floor. Heights of rooms gradually diminish upward from the ground, and the string-courses that

ZUTPHEN, GELDERLAND (DATED 1547)

VEERE, ZEELAND

externally mark the position of the floors, are consequently nearest together far up the walls and gables.

It will be seen by the foregoing how construction and practical arrangement went hand in hand with design, neither one being divorced from the other. Especially is this demonstrated by the Gothic buildings and those which primarily betray a Gothic origin. The house from Middelburg (page 40) is given as an example. It is a highly successful piece of grouping, and the features show with admirable effect. The walls are of brickwork and the dressings of stone. On the gable-end bands of stone alternate with courses of bricks, while set back in the angle the well-placed turret, steep-roofed and soaring, dominates the composition. How accurately the value of horizontal and vertical elements was estimated, and how cunningly they were opposed to each other, will be observed. The gateway from Nijmegen (page 41) was conceived in much the same spirit as the above, and here again the turret was effectively employed. Both it and the pointed archway are in quite the Gothic manner; but the crow-stone, or terminating member of the gable, the band of diaper executed in brick and stone, and the details of the windows (near to which the date of 1606 appears) point to other influences.

HAARLEM, NORTH HOLLAND

45

DELFT, SOUTH HOLLAND

46

HAARLEM, NORTH HOLLAND (DATED 1637)

ALKMAAR, NORTH HOLLAND (DATED 1673)

48

FRANEKER, FRIESLAND (DATED 1634)

CORBEL FROM DORDRECHT

On the exterior walls of the house from Zutphen (page 43) can be seen the sunk panels, set back from the main face of the brickwork, which served for the insertion of windows. They often extend from near the ground to well up the gable. The dividing projections, turned with arches at their extremities, give bold upright lines. In the example cited these lines have evidently been broken by the rebuilding of the first-storey wall. It is dated 1547. The upper part, showing the sunk panel bordered by moulded bricks, the arched head—in this instance pointed and supported on each side by small circular turrets—and the shuttered window, is given in detail on page 42.

A noticeable treatment of the ground floor elevation is exemplified by the two drawings from Alkmaar and Hoorn (pages 33 and 34), already considered, and by that from Veere (page 44). Each is constructed principally in woodwork, and the many windows amply serve to light the lofty rooms. The wooden mullions are simply shaped and enriched, while over them is a moulded cornice. Above the lower series of windows in the Alkmaar example is a projecting hood, which affords protection from the weather. The date of 1609 is carved upon it, and other buildings having this characteristic usually belong to the opening years of the seventeenth century. A more artistic and satisfactory solution to the difficult problem of adequately lighting the entire side of a high room or shop would not easily be found in the old work of any other country.

It is not possible to make any hard and fast division between Gothic and Renaissance work. The actual dates of the buildings form no conclusive key, for it has been demonstrated in the Introduction how the later development did not advance evenly throughout the country. Houses built in the traditional way, and in a mixture of styles, are to be seen in almost all old towns (page 45). Sometimes one influence shows predominantly, sometimes another. The brick and stone façade at Delft (page 46) has all the attributes

MOSAIC BRICK AND STONE WORK FROM DORDRECHT (see opposite page).

DORDRECHT, SOUTH HOLLAND (DATED 1608)

WORKUM, FRIESLAND (DATED 1663)

52

ARNHEM, GELDERLAND (DATED 1642)

AMSTERDAM—REMBRANDT'S HOUSE (DATED 1606)

ZWOLLE, OVERIJSSEL—THE GUILD HALL (DATED 1571)

VLISSINGEN (FLUSHING), ZEELAND (DATED 1614)

of Gothic work, pointed arches, overhanging stories, stepped gable and pinnacles. But the spirit of the carved details is different. The heads in circles, cherubs, vases, cornucopias, lion-heads, dolphins, eagles and acanthus ornament are all subjects far removed from Gothic ideas, as are the delicately carved corbels from which the arches spring.

Two other houses that owe much to Gothic influences are those from Haarlem (page 47) and Alkmaar (page 48). The first-named was built in 1637 and the second in 1673. The more recently dated example shows, in point of style, the earlier architectural form. Both have the customary stepped gable and window-heads, the Alkmaar examples being elliptically arched and those at Haarlem pointed. But in the latter instance the keystones are furnished with Renaissance ornaments, as is the crowning pediment of the gable.

The three following buildings mark a further step forward in architectural development. In general disposition of masses they accord with olden practices, but the decorative details approximate Renaissance ideas. " De Crimpert Salm " at Dordrecht (page 51), of 1608, presents a rich appearance, but the profuse elaboration of the front was not achieved by accident or haphazard use of material. The balance of the design was obviously well considered. Horizontal motives, intensified below the

DORDRECHT, SOUTH HOLLAND (DATED 1626)

KAMPEN, OVERIJSSEL (DATED 1631)

58

KAMPEN, OVERIJSSEL (DATED ON DORMERS 1634, 1626, 1730, 1630, AND 1619)

GRONINGEN—THE "GOUDKANTOOR" (DATED 1635)

GRONINGEN (1661)

61

FRANEKER, FRIESLAND (DATED 1662)

’S HERTOGENBOSCH, NORTH BRABANT (DATED 1671)

first-floor level, give a stable base for the lavishness overhead; above, they repeat with less force and are finally carried up the gable by the steps. The vertical lines, obtained principally by the window openings and frames, are similarly reduced towards the top, and there the curved elements are concentrated. Upon a low wall of stone and brick stands the woodwork front of the ground floor. Next in order comes a broad band of mosaic decoration executed in brick and stone (page 50), bounded at each end by lion-heads in high relief, and divided centrally by a stone panel with a salmon carved upon it. Other mosaics show in the arched spaces over the windows of the next storey (page 50), while the equivalent space in the gable is filled with arranged brickwork. Moulded bricks and stonework, plain and carved, all contribute to the exuberance of the scheme. The small example from Franeker (page 49) is built in brick and stone and was erected in 1634. It has the traditional gable but the old type of step, small in height and width, was not followed. Two steps only suffice to reach the gable-head and the side of each is finished with shaped stonework, a method of completion not employed in earlier times. Later in date than these two houses, that from Workum (page 52) gives an instance both of the persistence of established practice and of the human desire for newness and change. The builder evidently could neither forget nor abandon the general form of house arrangement that he knew so well, and to it he kept. This is especially obvious in the gable which mounts up in quite the Gothic way. The pilasters on the ground and first storey, however, plainly show that an attempt was made to keep in touch with the prevailing mode of the period. Each is terminated by a Corinthian capital and festoons of fruit are carved upon the panels. In these particulars the work, which was completed in 1663, was in agreement with the then advancing Classic taste. The bricks used in the walls are plum coloured and measure but $1\frac{1}{4}$ inches wide.

Designers were thus getting farther away from Gothic architecture. The political and religious events of the sixteenth and seventeenth centuries revolutionized old beliefs. Time-honoured faiths were not only given up, but were viewed with positive distrust. The powers that had swayed the people of the Middle Ages, the mysticism, ideals, and poetry of their lives, were unrealities to the great majority of seventeenth-century Hollanders; such doctrines fell meaningless upon their senses, and were to them but unintelligible and empty forms. They not unnaturally turned from a creed in whose name loathsome crimes had been committed and countless lives had been sacrificed. It was a time of new life and faith. This

IRON WALL-TIE FROM ALKMAAR (see opposite page)

ALKMAAR, NORTH HOLLAND (DATED 1672)

change in the trend of thought is amply reflected in the domestic architecture. The Gothic tradition, already more or less alienated from the public sympathies, had almost spent itself. Its vitality was gone and only as a survival, a mere shadow of former glory, was it carried on. The old order gave place to the new. But it was long before a fresh system of planning came to be generally accepted and mediæval methods of construction and workmanship still persisted. Classic motives, however, were increasingly applied to the elevations. All the features, and the entire decoration of many of the houses, were often the direct outcome of Renaissance influences. In some few cases—such as the gateway at Arnhem of 1642 (page 53)—the whole schemes were conceived in the Classic spirit and were evidently designed by men of advanced intelligence, who were able to comprehend the significance of the style in which they worked.

Rembrandt's house at Amsterdam (page 54) is an able achievement, sober and dignified. The walls are built of ochre-coloured bricks, with stone used for the dressings. The date of 1606 appears on the upper storey. It has no gabled front, but a projecting cornice and pediment make division between the roof and wall surface. Above are two dormers placed in balanced order; while the roof, steeply rising and hipped and having a chimney at each end of the ridge, completes the studied arrangement. So far the work is in the style of the Renaissance, and it is only by the windows below that earlier influences are recalled: but the two themes are so well blended as to be perfectly harmonious. The net result is simple and reasonable and by no means lacking in scholarship. Very different is the Guild Hall at Zwolle (page 55), erected thirty-five years earlier. Its too fussy elaboration is in sharp contrast with the comparative

'S GRAVENHAGE (THE HAGUE), SOUTH HOLLAND—"T'GOUTSMITS KEUR HUIJS"

VELSEN, NORTH HOLLAND

SPAARWOUDE, NORTH HOLLAND

restraint of Rembrandt's house, just mentioned. Classicism was applied without the Classic spirit and with little understanding of its real import. The general effect is rich and complex, but the composition lacks breadth and is overladen with ornament. Some of the details disclose good craftsmanship, notably the frieze which runs across the entire front at the first floor level, carved with cupids on horseback, old men with tridents, satyrs and flowing foliage, and broken at intervals by lion-heads worked on the bases of the pilasters. At the second storey is a Doric frieze, with sculptured circular ornaments and heads of bulls appearing in the metopes between the triglyphs. The gable, mediæval in feeling, is curly in outline ; it is further complicated by the introduction of reclining satyrs and lascivious demi-gods that quaintly break the skyline. The designer evidently proposed to himself the Italian ideal, but did not grasp the meaning or refinement of it. Many details came to be used in a similar way, such, for instance, as those shown from Dordrecht (page 50) and Flushing (page 56), but, although often of admirable workmanship, they were never coherent parts of a self-evolved whole.

A house of somewhat unusual appearance is that in the Voorstraat at Dordrecht, dated 1626 and illustrated on page 57. At the top is an open arcade constructed wholly in bricks, with the exception of the stones upon which the arches rest. The brick walls are relieved by stonework, while projecting pilasters separate the large lead-glazed and shuttered windows.

Houses that depended upon dormers for their controlling architectural idea were common in the seventeenth century. The front wall is usually only one storey high and the dormers rise from it at the line of the eaves. When the frontage is wide and the building long and low, as is the case at Kampen (page 59), these features—shaped and carved and fundamentally valuable in lighting the rooms of the roof—show with good effect. A smaller house in the same town, given on page 58, has a single dormer only. It contributes the necessary interest to what would otherwise be a very dull effort of building. On the frieze at its base is a carved stone representation of the Nativity, while below appears the inscription "IN BETHLEHEM 1631."

ZUTPHEN, GELDERLAND

HALFWEG, NORTH HOLLAND

Those principles that imparted to the domestic architecture of Holland its picturesqueness, and so gave to it its most valued possession, were strained to the uttermost as the freshness of the Transitional style declined. The influences bequeathed from former ages were running out. Extreme freedom of design, although showing certain originality and character, was not accompanied by necessary restraint. Architects sometimes cast aside all the limitations of their art and gave themselves up to unreasonable over-elaboration and the grotesque ; they ignored the fact—true for all time—that construction must form the basis for ornamental detail. But it must not be thought that this was always so. There is, however, certain work of this period that cannot seriously be accepted as good. Brickwork and stone continued to be employed and were still associated with excellent workmanship, as was the carpentry. There was evidently yet, as the many dated buildings prove, a large body of men who had complete mastery of their particular crafts, men versed in that traditional skill which had come down unbrokenly from mediæval days. Prominence was given to the numerous door and window openings, which were heavily

HALFWEG, NORTH HOLLAND
SHOWING CONSTRUCTION OF FARMHOUSE

SPAARNDAM, NORTH HOLLAND

SCHOOTEN, NORTH HOLLAND

moulded and often surmounted by pediments. Gables were shaped in endless ways and upon them almost every conceivable combination of curves was employed. Pilasters and cornices, swags and festoons, with strap ornament, scrolls and ornate iron wall-ties, all generally of debased Renaissance character, contributed to the rich profusion.

Whither events in architectural history were tending will be seen in the following illustrations. The " Goudkantoor " at Groningen (page 60), bearing a motto and date of 1635, and a house near to it of the year 1661 (page 61), have quaint gables, curiously shaped and laden with carved stone decorations. On the walls below the same complex treatment continues, especially on the "Goudkantoor," the entrance doorway of which is emphasised by the work surrounding it. At Franeker (page 62) is an extreme development of the step gable, with the four steps supporting masses of coarsely-designed ornamentation. The heavy pediments to the windows are conspicuous, as are the many stone details. Two panels are inscribed with " ANNO 1662." With the above-mentioned may be compared the two gables at Alkmaar (page 65) which betray the same source of origin. Each is crowned by a stone pediment, and the steps have carvings resting upon them. Applied to the wall of the farthermost house, and placed centrally between the windows of the second storey, is a notable iron wall-tie of much larger size than was usual. An enlarged drawing of it is reproduced on page 64. Another variation of gable outline is illustrated from 's Hertogenbosch

THE FERRY-HOUSE, NEAR GENNEP, NORTH BRABANT

BEEK, GELDERLAND

(page 63). In this case the stone-capped sides follow the lines of sweeping curves, and on them, facing outwardly, are little carved bunches of fruit and flowers. The front face of this building is remarkable for the use of pilasters. They are boldly carried up from bases to the head of the gable. The pillars, executed in unrelieved brickwork, have stone capitals of the Ionic order which carry an entablature. There appears the date of MDCLXXI. The bricks are 2 inches wide by 9 inches long and are laid about five courses to one foot.

It eventually came to pass that the gabled treatment, which had been the guiding principle of house design for so many generations, was given up. And with the disappearance of it there went that which had given character to the architecture of Holland. The links of the tradition were broken. The old sources of inspiration no longer served. Inherited ability and skill, originality and vigour, were being lost, and the last traces of native ideas are to be found in inconspicuous buildings such as that given from The Hague (page 66). Although hipped roofs, wide projecting cornices and other Renaissance features were employed, as is shown by the drawings from Velsen (page 67), and Zutphen (page 69), a pure Renaissance domestic architecture did not become established. When the traditional style, owning both Gothic and Renaissance motives, had ceased to

BRIGDAMME, ZEELAND (DATED 1622)

BEEK, GELDERLAND

hold its ground, the stream of design—which until then had flowed continuously—ebbed low, and houses became uninteresting and commonplace.

Away in the country the town architecture is mirrored in the brick buildings of the numerous villages. Less pretentious in appearance, their style is well suited to the simpler conditions that there obtain ; for the crowded activity of the town waterways is absent on the calm canals that wind between meadows, and give communication from village to village ; on the quays life moves placidly. Spaarndam (page 71) furnishes a typical village view, with its gabled brick and white-fronted houses, screened by delicate greenery. The Ferry House, near Gennep (page 73), has more ornate gables, curved and stepped, and on the front is diaper brickwork.

There also developed a type of building peculiar to the countryside. It is shown by the many farmhouses and cottages. Their outward forms were determined by constructional principles, and added adornment was but little employed. They are unobtrusive examples of honest work, not claiming especial distinction, yet in thorough harmony with their natural environment. They were brought into being by prevailing needs, and are the local representatives of that phase of native art which is to be found in almost every country. Such village homes exist in all parts of Holland. The style of them shows little variation in the different localities. They

BLOEMENDAAL, NORTH HOLLAND

BROEK, NORTH HOLLAND

are equally suited to the windswept Friesland landscape, the watered provinces of North and South Holland, or the beautiful country of North Brabant, with its hedgerows and woods and distant hills. Grouping, perchance, around old brick churches and sheltered by trees, as at Spaarwoude (page 68), they are pleasant and rustic to see.

Under one great thatched or tiled roof all the covered accommodation necessary for farm life is contained. One side of the building is occupied by living apartments, the remainder providing a huge barn, stalls for cattle, and other conveniences for the farmer's work. These buildings were solidly constructed on a timber basis in the manner shown by the sectional view from Halfweg (page 70), where centre and side aisles are divided from each other by the stout upright timbers. Extreme durability was the keynote and the materials were employed according to their quality. This traditional form of building, practised for many generations, continues in use to the present day. An illustration of the exterior of a similar homestead to that mentioned above, and from the same village, also appears on page 70. The great roof, hipped at each end and covered with pantiles, will be observed. Beneath the eaves are the domestic rooms, in this instance all upon the ground floor ; often they extend to a second storey in the roof, which is then lighted by dormers. The cottages follow the same general constructive principles as the farms, and have similar low walls and large roofs. A lean-to was frequently added to give an additional room, and the main roof brought down over it at a less steep pitch. The roof space, valuable as a store, is in many cases reached from the exterior by a ladder. In addition to the customary steeply-pitched roofs, those of the Mansard pattern occur less frequently, as is exemplified by the drawing from Schooten (page 72).

Country work does not exhibit a great variety of building materials. Bricks, being made from the natural product and consequently readily available, were principally used for the walls. Rather than left in their normal state, they were often thinly coated with plaster on the outer face, and the lower parts, for about two feet upwards from the ground, were tarred. Houses

BROEK, NORTH HOLLAND

WELL AT BEUGEN, NORTH BRABANT

and cottages of this description together form a characteristic group in the country architecture of Holland. They were built upon a traditional system which grew out of the accumulated experience that was transmitted from generation to generation. Customary examples are shown in the two drawings from Beek (pages 74 and 76), and by that from Broek in Waterland (page 78). The farmhouse from Brigdamme (page 75) is of a similar character; at the entrance are two stone gate-piers, dated 1622. Two influences are to be traced in the farm at Bloemendaal (page 77). The main building has the white plastered walls and large roof—which in this case comes forward to cover an open verandah—while the adjoining gable is of natural coloured bricks and more in the style of town work.

Houses with wooden walls are prevalent, especially in North Holland. Upon a low brick wall, tarred, and varying in height from 18 to 30 inches, the timber frame was erected. Boards were simply nailed to it and the framing was commonly left exposed to view on the exterior. The boarding was well coated with paint or tar for protection against the weather. A roof of thatch or tiles, well projecting at the eaves, covered the whole. There was thus provided, by simple and economical means, a type of building well suited for its purpose. The village of Broek has many examples of timber houses, such as those here given on page 79; while near by, at Monnikendam, Volendam, and on the Island of Marken, are numerous others.

BEEK, GELDERLAND

BRIDGE AT ZUIDERWOUDE, NORTH HOLLAND (DATED 1799)

An extravagant use of paint is conspicuous in the country as well as the towns. It is renewed at frequent intervals and, in the main, it is well applied. Shutters and doors and window frames, and frequently the whole house front, are freely covered with it. But the effects are not unpleasing. They give to the villages an air of gaiety and freshness. Plain schemes of colour are wisely adhered to, while throughout a district one general note will be followed. On the island of Walcheren it is apple-green and white ; north of Amsterdam bluey-green and cream ; while the woodwork of the house at Beek (page 81) is painted in the tones of buff that find favour in the locality of Nijmegen.

There are many other domestic features worthy of note to be seen in the villages of Holland ; quaint appliances for wells, ingeniously worked (page 80), or little bridges that span dividing dykes, and connect homesteads with the highways. One from Zuiderwoude, near the edge of the Zuider Zee, is illustrated on this page. It is built of brick relieved by a little stonework. On the keystone of the arch appears the date of 1799. The wooden gates above give access to the farm and the fields. The Dutch, too, have a marked fondness for natural beauty, as is demonstrated by the skill they display in laying-out open spaces. All towns can show flower gardens and lawns, or old fortifications overlooked by gaunt watch-towers, transformed into pleasant parks. Nijmegen and Arnhem are noteworthy in this respect. Very charming, too, are the village streets, of which that at Brigdamme (page 18) is a typical instance. They are lined with many trees that afford kindly shade in summer and shelter from the wind, and gratify the eyes with traceries of green.

DIVISION II

EXTERIOR FEATURES—DOORS, WINDOWS, GABLES & ORNAMENTS

II.—EXTERIOR FEATURES—DOORS, WINDOWS, GABLES & ORNAMENTS.

FROM the time when Dutch houses were built in a definite recognised style the features were always treated with skill and care. The many and crowded openings were accentuated. Doorways became imposing through the enrichment that surrounded them and windows were similarly emphasised. Panels, carvings, and ironwork decorated the walls, while the crowning gables, crow-stepped or curved, completed the richness of the buildings. Upon all these details, whether for a public building or private dwelling, great labour was expended. A careful examination of them discloses much inventive readiness and meritorious execution.

Particular prominence was given to external doorways. The manner of their treatment varied widely. They were regarded as more than mere ways of access and upon them the best skill of the craftsmen was frequently concentrated. A personal note would be added by the introduction of the owner's arms or initials, the date of the work, or some quaint conceit of peculiar and subtle meaning. Among the examples extant, those of the early period incline to greatest simplicity. They were based on the current forms that were employed in ecclesiastical and civic architecture. The openings are spacious and are surrounded by mouldings. The arches at the heads are pointed, trefoil, or elliptic shapes. When there are label - mouldings above they follow the

WOUDRICHEM, NORTH BRABANT (DATED 1611)

LEEUWARDEN, FRIESLAND

curves of the arches and support or surround the arms, panels, or other decorations.

The doorway at Delft (page 87) is a good example of work dictated by Gothic influences. From carved stops at each side spring the simple mouldings that extend round the opening. It is surmounted by a label, near the centre of which is a three-sided space, enclosed by mouldings and filled by a winged cherub's head carved in relief, while the label is terminated by a finial. The wooden door is noteworthy. It is composed of six boards and upon the outer face of each are shallow grooves running continuously from top to bottom. Projecting nailheads arranged in vertical lines, together with other ironwork, give further interesting ornamentation. Another doorway from the same town (page 88) is built of stone and moulded bricks. The space at the head, contained within a trefoil arch, has carved upon it a shield—lacking armorial bearings—supporters, and a scroll with the date of 1547. The semi-circular arch which surrounds the trefoil is one of the series that repeat across the building. That other early type of house, peculiar for its windowed ground floor front constructed in wood,

DELFT, SOUTH HOLLAND

87

DELFT, SOUTH HOLLAND (DATED 1547)

"THE MIRROR." FROM AN OIL PAINTING BY CATHERINE BISSCHOP-SWIFT.

(In the Municipal Museum, Amsterdam.)

NIJMEGEN, GELDERLAND. FROM A WATER-COLOUR DRAWING BY SYDNEY R. JONES.

HAARLEM, NORTH HOLLAND (DATED 1632)

LEEUWARDEN, FRIESLAND (DATED 1675)

LEIDEN, RHIJNLAND (DATED 1612)

such as is given from Veere on page 44, had its entrance doorway made with three plain stout timbers, one at each side and one across the top as a lintel. An elaboration of the simple wooden doorway occurs at Leiden (page 89). It is crowned by mouldings, below which appears an ogee arch shaped in wood. The parti-coloured effect of the door itself is achieved by the application of contrasting tints of paint.

The circular arch followed the pointed although simultaneously a modified form of the latter, of which that from Haarlem (page 89) is an instance, continued to be used. Of circular-arched doorways there are endless examples which were erected in a manner that became general and customary. They were usually built in stone and bricks. Those from Leiden (below), Flushing (page 91), and Leeuwarden (page 86) are characteristic. The Leiden doorway of 1615, with moulded opening and carved archstones, is doubtless the earliest of the three and most nearly allied to the work of the preceding century. The two remaining examples incline to later influences, particularly to be observed in the enrichment of the jambs.

Changing taste brought a new treatment to external doorways. They were affected by the same forces that altered the outward character of late sixteenth and seventeenth-century houses. Renaissance detail gradually became established and doorways of the seventeenth-century were frankly treated in a Classic way, rich in pilasters, capitals, friezes, pediments and mouldings, with an especial preference for an adapted form of the Ionic order. Stone was now almost exclusively used for this feature, unaccompanied by brick. "Delvitt's Poort" at Woudrichem (page 85) shows a rather advanced development for the period of 1611 to which it belongs. The whole of it is painted, with the carved details picked out in different colours. Two doorways illustrated here are

LEIDEN, RHIJNLAND (DATED 1615)

VLISSINGEN (FLUSHING), ZEELAND

well designed and proportioned. They are distinguished by the elaboration that appears at their heads. Upon the frieze immediately above the arch of the Kampen example (page 93) will be seen the inscription and date of 1665, over which is a broken pediment surmounted by particularly well-rendered armorial bearings carved in stone. The frieze at Leeuwarden (page 89) is similarly inscribed, the date in this case being 1675, while within the heavily moulded pediment is a coat of arms. Less complicated is the doorway from Leiden of 1655 (page 96). It is crowned by mouldings and decorated below by festoons in relief. The above will show the fashion of the time, tending towards correctness in design, with details carefully thought out and well executed.

Many eighteenth-century doorways were unduly florid and may well be described as rococo. That from Marssum in Friesland (below), belonging to the year 1713, is of this kind. The overladen ornament and peculiarities of design suggest the unreality of a poor stage-setting, rather than serious architecture; while the incongruity of the work can only be appreciated by an inspection of the original, situated as it is among cottages in a quiet village street. Later in the century French influence was predominant. Details, such as are noticeable in the Arnhem doorway (page 94), were based on the Louis XV. style which not only affected the work of the towns but permeated into the heart of the country. The small cottage doors and doorways in villages such as Broek have all the attributes of the then prevailing mode.

The wooden doors were much enriched either with applied ironwork, or mouldings and panels. Metal locks, bolts, hinges and nails are conspicuous in the early specimens. The use of ironwork on the door from Dordrecht (page 95) is carried to an extreme degree ; but, be it noted, all the fittings

MARSSUM, FRIESLAND (DATED 1713)

KAMPEN, OVERIJSSEL (DATED 1665)

have a practical purpose. It was only after needs had been provided for that embellishment was added, discernible in the shaping of the lock-plates and hinges and the arrangement of the nailheads. The centre of the more recent example from Haarlem (page 95) is occupied by a large sunk panel surrounded by mouldings, a section of which is given. A good piece of woodcarving is that appearing on the lintel, having for its subject a ship sailing on rough water.

Windows of houses were almost always square-headed. They appear so in existing examples belonging to the Gothic period. The traceries and pointed heads, usual in early civic buildings, were rarely adopted for house windows, although arched spaces, filled with tracery, were not uncommonly built over them. A fine series of such window-heads is to be seen on the stone front of the "Scotch House" at Veere (page 97); there are others at Kampen and on a house in the Groenmarkt at Dordrecht. Except in cases where the openings were small, they were divided vertically by mullions and transversely by cross-bars. The lower windows were closed by wooden shutters. Two examples, from Nijmegen and Dordrecht (page 99), both of Gothic design and of sixteenth century workmanship, are illustrated. The Dordrecht shutter is constructed of beautifully grained pieces of oak, jointed and pegged together.

Late Gothic windows have also pointed and elliptical arches over the heads unenriched by decoration. They were customarily built in brickwork, with the window spaces flush, or set back from the face of the walling. Pointed arches ceased to be generally used after the coming of the Renaissance. The elliptical shape, however, continued, and the establishment of the circular arch was but a short and natural step in development. These two forms obtained for many succeeding years. Instances of either type are presented in the drawing from Zwolle (page 101), and innumerable others are shown by the illustrations in this volume. They were not given up until displaced by classic pediments, or the overhead feature was altogether abandoned. The gabled

ARNHEM, GELDERLAND

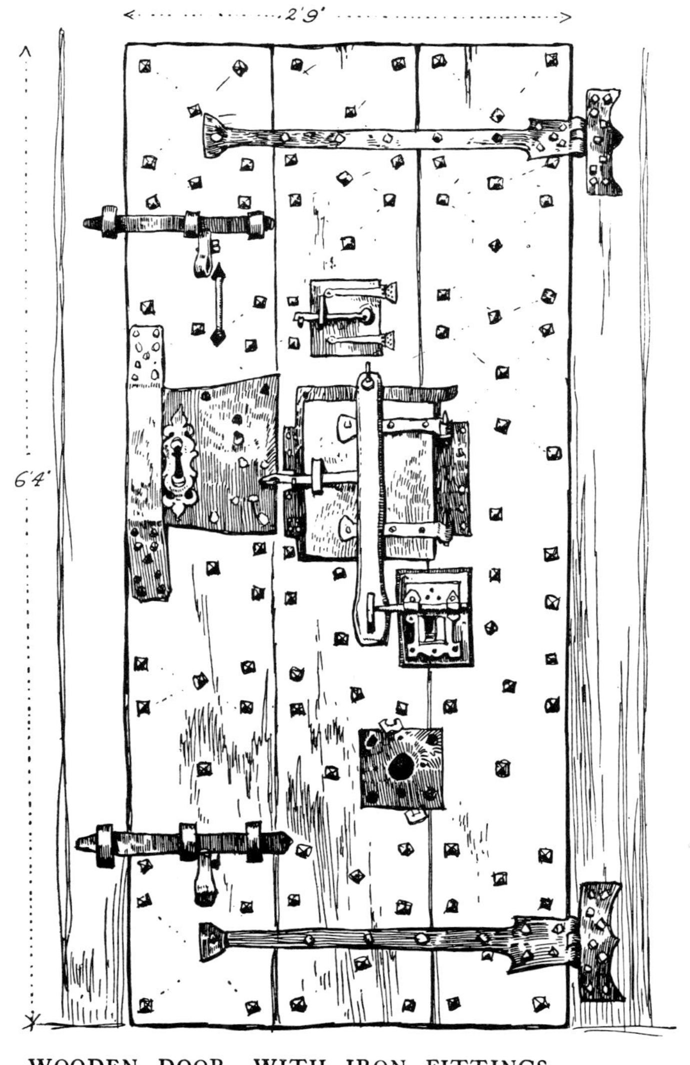

WOODEN DOOR, WITH IRON FITTINGS,
FROM DORDRECHT, SOUTH HOLLAND

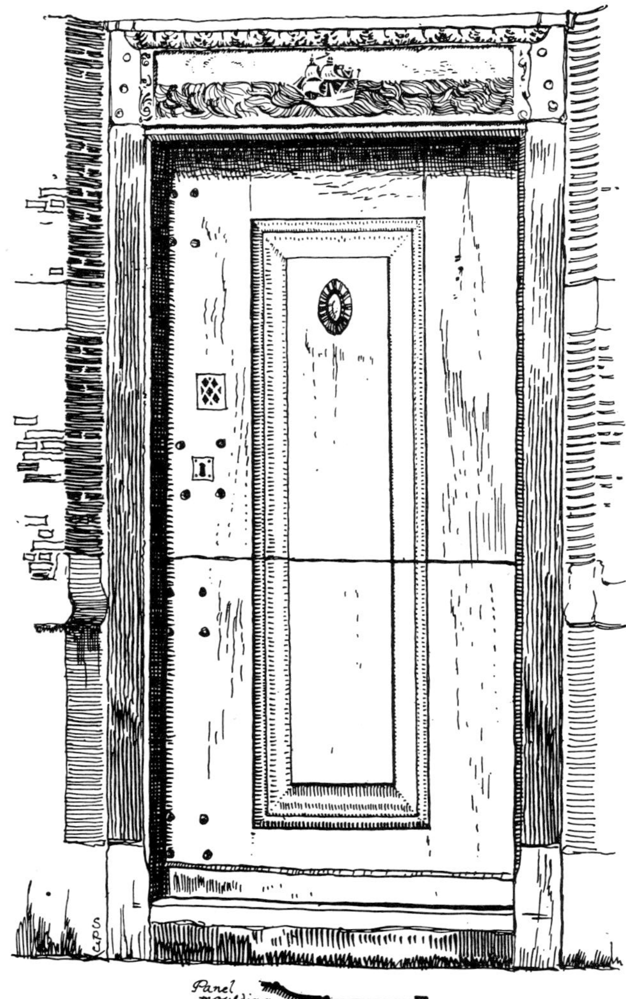

WOODEN DOOR, WITH CARVED LINTEL,
FROM HAARLEM, NORTH HOLLAND

LEIDEN, RHIJNLAND (DATED 1655)

96

VEERE, ZEELAND—THE "SCOTCH HOUSE"

WOODEN WINDOW-FRAME, WITH IRON FITTINGS AND LEAD GLAZING, FROM DORDRECHT, SOUTH HOLLAND

front at Gorinchem (page 103), built in stone and brick, has circular arches appearing over the windows. The enclosed spaces are richly decorated by stone carvings, and the character of the work seems to be advanced for the period to which it apparently belongs. Much interesting sculpture is also distributed over the gable and walls of this building.

Windows were first glazed with leaded lights. Small squares of glass, as at Dordrecht (page 98), or diamond panes were used. But during the seventeenth century the employment of wooden bars became universal and leadwork went out of fashion. The openings were divided centrally by transoms, the lower windows receding inwards considerably more than the upper ones.

Wooden shutters, opening outwards, were still customary. They were occasionally large enough to cover the whole window, but usually only the lower half was furnished with them. Seventeenth-century shutters are not comparable, in point of carved enrichment, with those of Gothic times ; the woodwork, frequently devoid of ornament, is fastened to the window-frames by iron strap-hinges, and fitted with bolts and catches. They are, however, brightly painted and are interesting in consequence, giving colour to the architectural groups. Many harmonious schemes are to be observed ; green and white ; white, green and red ; yellow and black ; red and black ; and numerous others. The coloured drawing from Nijmegen (opposite) shows shutters painted in red and black ; while several specimens, from North and South Holland, are given (pages 98 to 100). The glazing of windows was first enclosed by casements, with hinges to open and shut. After casements came sash windows, which

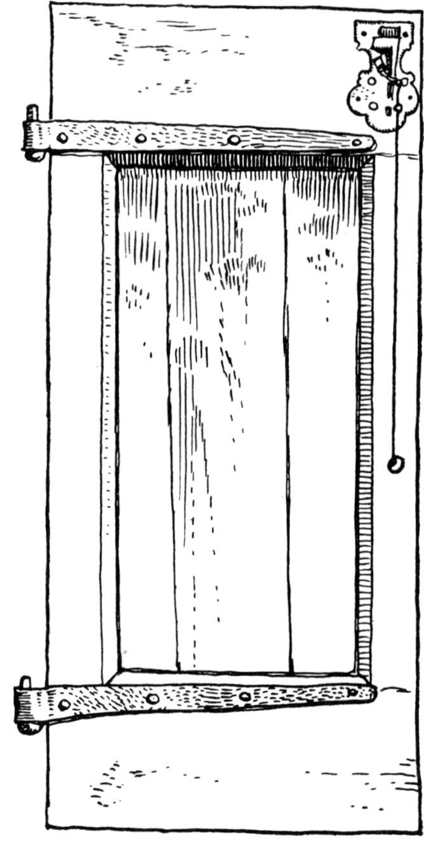

WINDOW SHUTTER FROM VELSEN

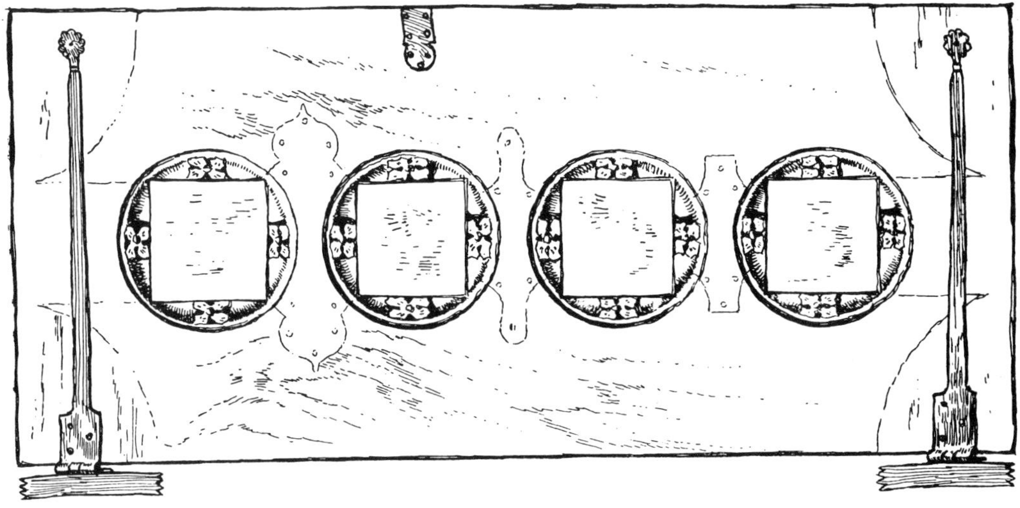

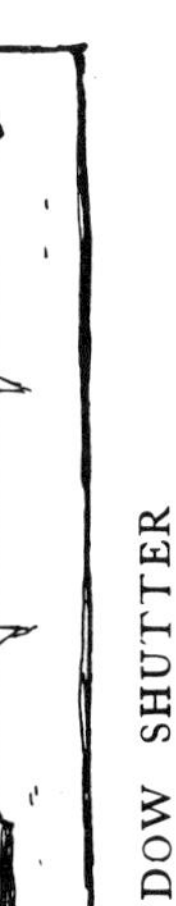

WINDOW SHUTTER FROM DORDRECHT

WINDOW SHUTTERS FROM LEIDEN

WINDOW SHUTTER FROM NIJMEGEN

were substituted for the older form. There are many shown in the illustrations. Those from Flushing (page 105), appearing on a house dated 1625, differ somewhat from the usual type, being surrounded by mouldings and carvings. Dormer windows also, as has already been stated, became much-developed features during the seventeenth and eighteenth centuries. Three characteristic specimens are given: two from Kampen, of the years 1626 and 1634, and a later dormer, from Marssum, belonging to the eighteenth century, all shown on page 102.

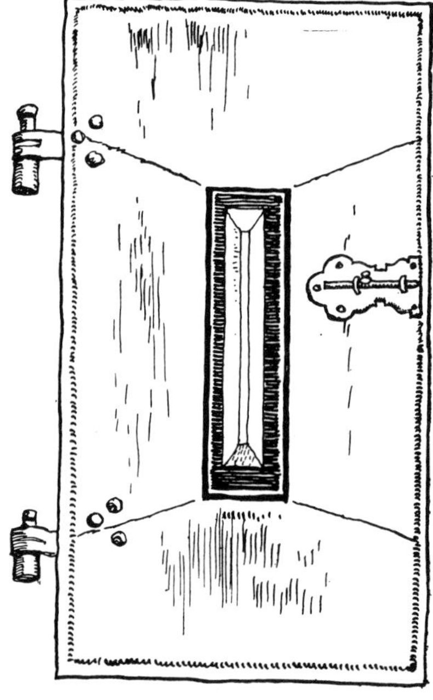

WINDOW SHUTTER FROM HAARLEM

The distinguishing gables—so often mentioned, and intimately associated with house development—exhibit infinite varieties of treatment. Between the early stepped shapes, and the fantastic outlines of later days, there is an innumerable succession. They followed the trend of design prevalent at the time of their erection. Thus, the two gables, from Kampen (page 104) and Dordrecht (page 107), are in keeping with the current forms of the late Gothic period. They are both built of stone and decorated on the face with sunk panels and carvings. The Kampen gable has pinnacles rising from the coping of the steps, usual features in work of the time; while the twisted finials at Dordrecht, associated with the first quarter of the sixteenth century, are worthy of notice.

WINDOW SHUTTER FROM MONNIKENDAM

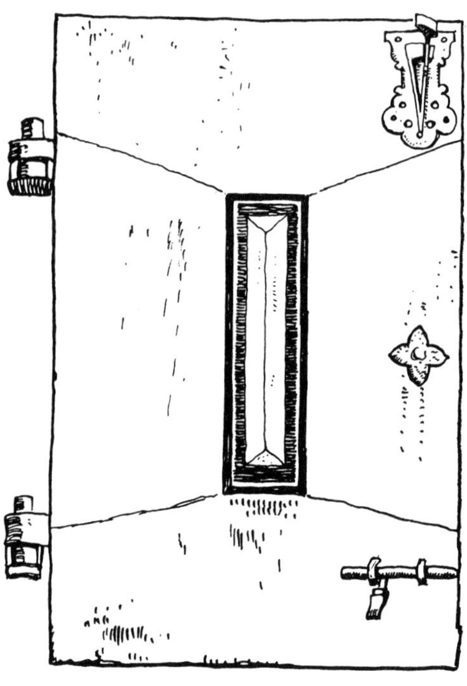

WINDOW SHUTTER FROM HAARLEM

It is impossible to consider here in detail

ZWOLLE, OVERIJSSEL

the numerous vicissitudes through which the development of the gable passed during the many years that Gothic and Renaissance motives were acting together as guiding influences. Roughly and briefly, mediæval character was observed in respect to construction and general management of masses—evident by the stepped and curved gables—with a marked tendency to Classic feeling in the handling of details. Work was carried out wholly in

KAMPEN, OVERIJSSEL
(DATED 1626)

MARSSUM, FRIESLAND

brick, or in brick relieved by stone. Among the large number of different outlines that are in evidence, those based on the original stepped form show predominantly. But the spirit of the times is discernible in the culminating pediments, mouldings, and stone decorations. Four typical gables, all sketched in North Holland, are illustrated (pages 106 and 109). A good example of shaping, achieved by the use of oppositive curves, is that from Arnhem (page 108), and the stonework of the copings extends to the strapwork ornament.

KAMPEN, OVERIJSSEL
(DATED 1634)

GORINCHEM (GORCUM), SOUTH HOLLAND (DATED 1566)

Two gables from Leiden (page 109) are well carried out in brickwork. How effectively window-heads and copings were handled, yet withal in a perfectly workmanlike way, is demonstrated by the larger drawing; the brickwork is flush and obliquely tailed into the horizontal courses of the wall.

Long sweeping curves were much employed in the shaping of later gables. The house opposite the bridge in the Franeker illustration (page 113) has such a gable, and it is dated 1735. Another, from Amsterdam (page 110), has similar characteristics. Both are enriched with stone representations of fruit and flowers, vases and festoons, all quite in the spirit of late seventeenth and eighteenth-century work.

The sides of the gables of farmhouses and country cottages, straight and unshaped, are not uncommonly protected by barge-boards. The two timbers, running from base to apex, may have mouldings worked at the edge of them; or the undersides are diversified by repeating curves, with pendants appearing at the lower ends. Both methods are figured in detail in drawings 1, 2, and 4 on page 111.

Fascia-boards, applied to overhanging stories of wooden houses, are similarly decorated; two are exemplified in numbers 6 and 7. The wooden finials, which are planted on the outer faces of the gables at their highest points, are variously shaped and perforated, and the details numbered 1, 2, 3 and 5 give four examples of them.

There is an absence of interesting chimneys in Holland, for the gable ends of the high and narrow-fronted houses, bordering the street, obscured from view these objects of usefulness. Solely utilitarian, therefore, they generally remained, shafts of the simplest form, serving the purpose for which they were devised, owing nothing to beauty or ornament and little to precedent. When hipped roofs were employed, instead of gables, chimneys came into greater prominence. But even then—with an absence of developed, traditional forms to give the basis for the evolution of a settled type—they did not constitute important decorative factors in the architectural scheme. Many stacks have neither mouldings

KAMPEN, OVERIJSSEL

(In the Ryks Museum, Amsterdam.)

"SEVENTEENTH-CENTURY DUTCH INTERIOR."
FROM AN OIL PAINTING BY BARON J. A. HENDRIK LEYS.

HINDELOOPEN ROOM AT THE FRISIAN MUSEUM, LEEUWARDEN. FROM A WATER-COLOUR DRAWING BY SYDNEY R. JONES.

VLISSINGEN (FLUSHING), ZEELAND

MONNIKENDAM, NORTH HOLLAND

nor other projection at the top. Chimneys a little more elaborate than was usual are shown by the two illustrations from Hoorn and Zutphen (page 112). They deviate somewhat from the plain rectangular shape, and both have moulded heads; while the Hoorn example has a pyramidal hood covered with lead and supported by four metal uprights.

Isolated stone ornaments are numerous. They were inserted into walls with freedom and wheresoever caprice or fancy suggested—high up on gables, around doorways, over windows, or distributed on what would otherwise have been unrelieved spaces. The rich appearance of the buildings is in no small measure due to the extravagant use of these details. That bizarre kind of ornament, known by the name of strapwork, and well shown in the Arnhem gable (page 108), was freely used, as was carved work based upon Italian motives. Among the latter may be mentioned the more or less conventional representation of human forms, fruit and flowers, birds, fishes and beasts, with prominence given to heads of lions, or the complete animal in the attitude sejeant, popularly used as a gable termination.

Of a more homely and personal character are the frequently occurring panels bearing, in well-cut figures and letters, dates, mottoes, and inscriptions; four are exemplified by the accompanying drawings from Zutphen (page 115) and Haarlem (pages 114 to 116). Equally symbolic of pride of home are the carved coats-of-arms which keep green, by visible sign, the

HAARLEM, NORTH HOLLAND

DORDRECHT, SOUTH HOLLAND (DATED 1523)

memory of the builder and the honour of his house. One such armorial decoration from Workum, dated 1644, is illustrated on page 115. All these little enrichments, so constantly seen, are more than mere examples of craftsmanship; they essentially express the sentiments of the man who caused the stones to be laid.

Things to be observed in everyday life naturally furnished subjects for carvings in stone. The forces of Nature, greatly influential in Holland—that is to say, water and wind and all that resulted therefrom—were turned to for inspiration. Decoratively treated water, with ships, windmills, and other appliances relevant to human convenience or suggestive of enterprise, were especially favoured. A windmill from Sneek, high in relief and painted black, red, gold and white, together with a ship from Haarlem

ARNHEM, GELDERLAND

appearing in an oval panel surrounded by a scrollwork frame, are illustrated (page 115). Interesting is the wall-panel at Franeker (page 114), with a scene from local history depicted upon it ; there is much spirit shown in the carving of the men and horses, while the water, drawbridge, and distant houses are well managed. The house known as "Inde Steenrotse," situated on the Dwars Quay at Middelburg, dated 1590, is noteworthy for its large panels in high relief. It was built by a wealthy mason. Five of the carved subjects portray various episodes connected with the working of stone and two are here given (page 116) ; others, higher up the building, represent biblical scenes from the Book of Exodus.

The mosaic decorations are of unusual interest, for they are of a kind more or less peculiar to this country. They were formed by inlaying small pieces of brick and stone set together to make repeating patterns or panels. As was customary, materials were used with just regard for their suitable adaptability to purpose; not employed unreasonably, or strained to accomplish

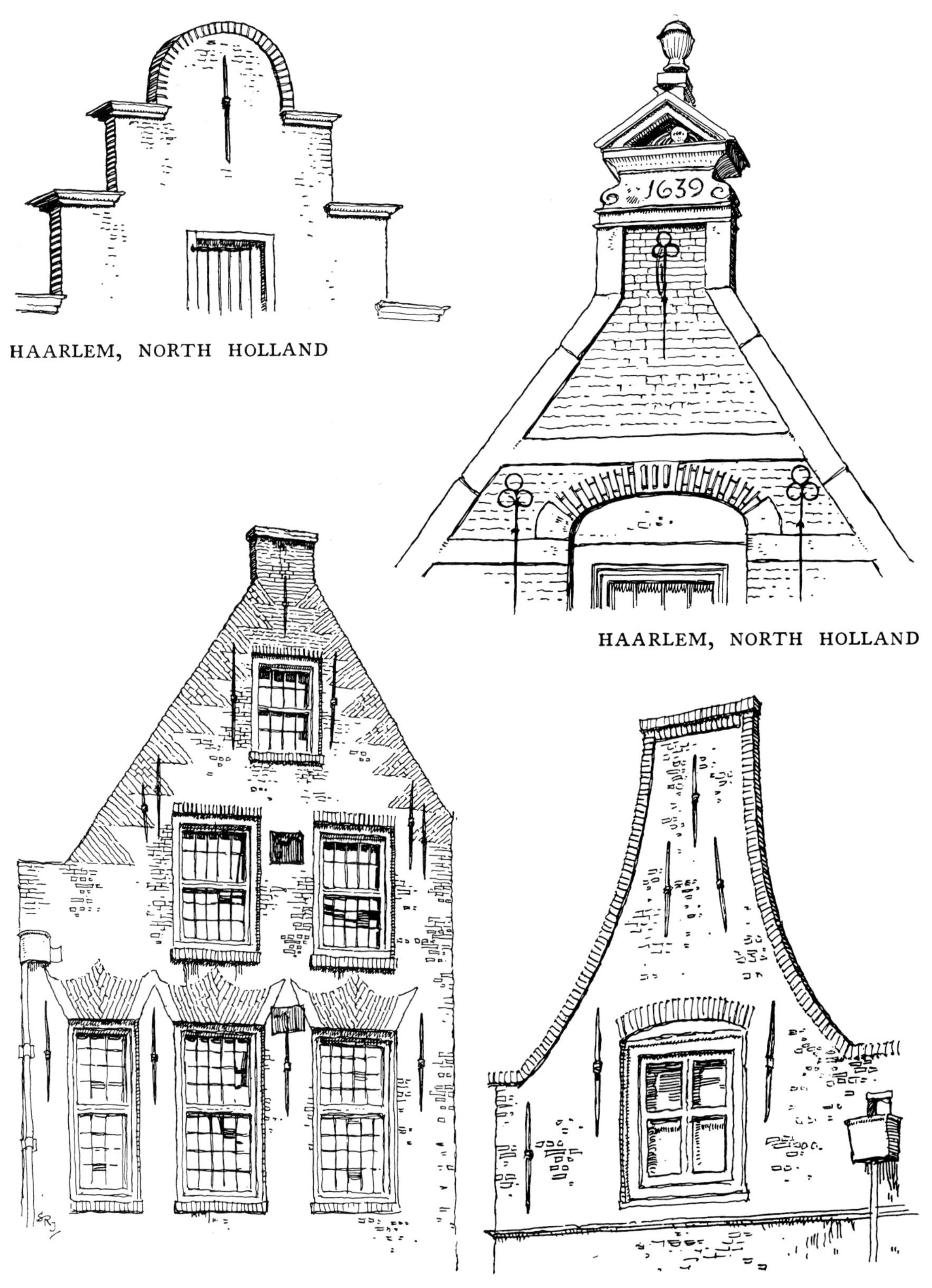

HAARLEM, NORTH HOLLAND

HAARLEM, NORTH HOLLAND

LEIDEN, RHIJNLAND

LEIDEN, RHIJNLAND

that for which they were not fitted. The units were simple and results legitimate. This ornamental work was principally used to enrich the arched spaces over window-heads ; less frequently it appears in bands carried horizontally across the buildings.

The houses at Woudrichem (page 117)—inscribed "Iden Salamander 1606" and "Zuden Gulden Engel 1593"—have notable examples of mosaics in the window-heads. Two of the patterns are shown in detail on page 118, together with two others from a house near by. All were achieved by manipulating little shaped pieces of brick to form devices, especially noticeable being the starlike figures with radiating points. Work of a similar kind appears on the house at Zwolle, dated 1609, and illustrated on page 119. An enlarged drawing of one of the window-heads (page 118) gives the precise arrangement of the brick and stonework. There is quite a Moorish feeling evident in this design, with the two main portions of inlay enclosed by arch-shaped lines curved horseshoe fashion. The horseshoe arch was essentially a product of Morocco, and the analogy with the East is further strengthened by the fact that mosaic was a medium extensively used by Byzantine and Saracenic artists. These circumstances all suggest the origin of the employment of such work in Holland.

On page 118 is represented a small section of the horizontal mosaic band that appears over the archway at Nijmegen (page 41). Simpler patterns were also formed with ordinary narrow bricks and mortar. Two examples are here given, both carried out in red and yellow bricks,—a frieze at the first storey level of a house at Workum and shaped spaces from Franeker (page 120).

Turning to external metalwork the most characteristic objects are the iron wall-ties. They were applied to walls to give them stability. But the possibilities for artistic treatment which the wall-ties offered were by no means overlooked, as is demonstrated by the many and varied forms produced by the blacksmiths, who regarded these accessories, before all things, as the particular field for the display of their skill. Endless varieties are to be found, certain patterns being local to specific districts. Upon ordinary houses—and they were practically invariably used—they are usually no more elaborate than might be achieved by direct work on the anvil ; of honest but unambitious appearance and shaped in simple ways, such as are shown by the illustrations on page 121.

AMSTERDAM, NORTH HOLLAND

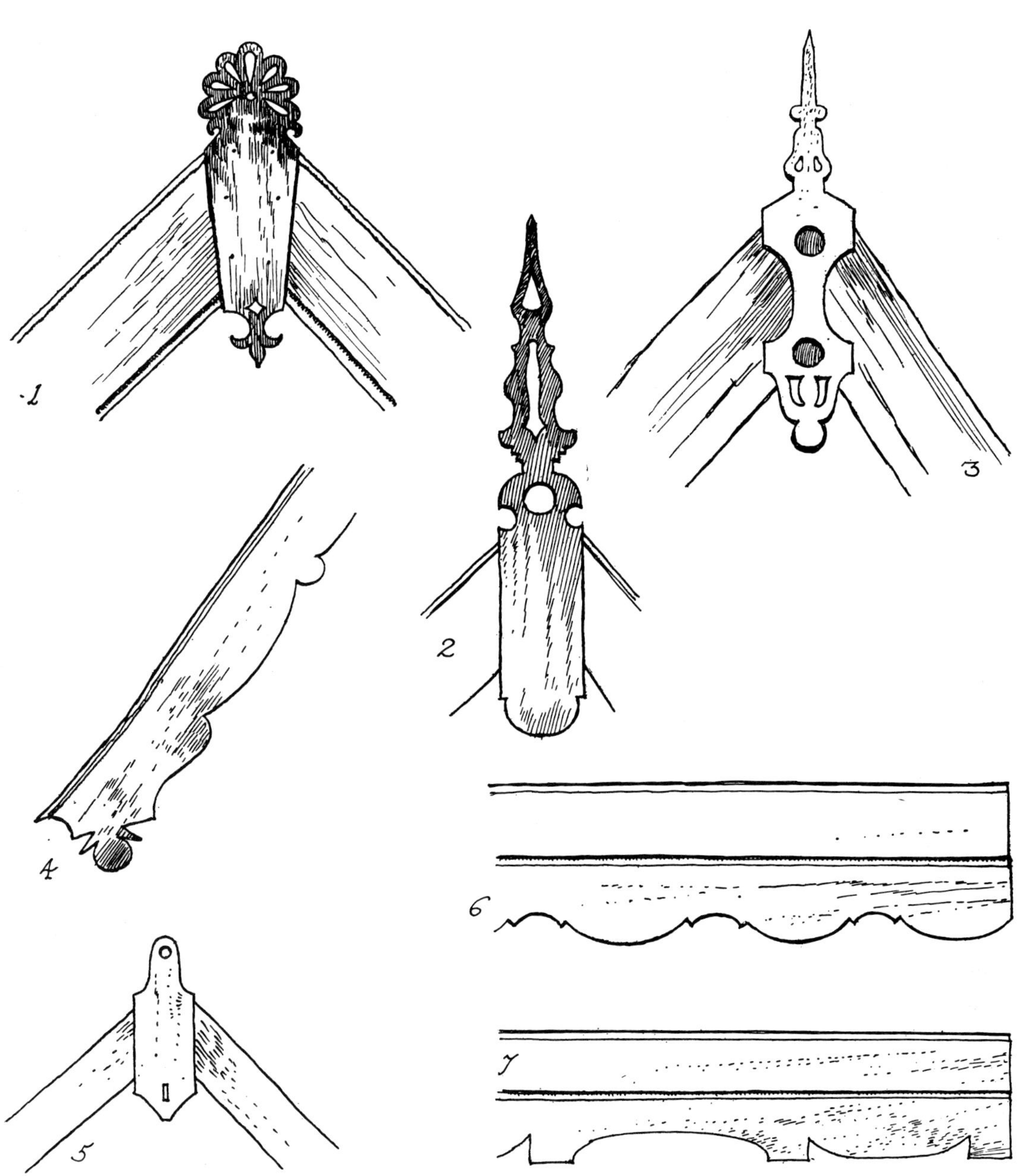

WOOD DETAILS FROM GELDERLAND AND SOUTH HOLLAND

But the wall-ties of more important buildings are often complicated affairs ; beautiful examples of design and craftsmanship which were wrought with labour. They are rich in scrolls and curves with foliated ornament, and one of the examples here given (page 123) has the date of 1798 worked within it. Iron letters and figures also decorate the fronts of many houses. Each is detached and secured to the wall by a single stay. They are arranged to denote dates or monograms. An example has already been seen at the base of a gable at Middelburg (page 35) ; another specimen, from St. Anna, near Nijmegen, is reproduced on page 122.

Other wrought ironwork was used for various purposes on doors and

windows, as well as to heighten the effect of certain features. A good instance of its application is demonstrated by the key-escutcheon, with supporting iron decorations, from Middelburg (page 123). The workmanship is of a traditional kind, with Gothic forms recalled by the cusps on the pierced plates. The iron door-knocker, appearing on the same page, is an interesting example of curious design and belongs to the sixteenth or seventeenth century. For windows, ironwork was used in the stout stay-bars and stanchions, instances of which, fitted to an oval opening, are furnished from Leiden (page 122).

ZUTPHEN, GELDERLAND

The magnificent wrought vanes of Holland, surmounting lofty belfries on public buildings, are justly famous and are reflected in the less elaborate shapes that adorn the roof points or gable terminations of business and dwelling-houses. One, from Middelburg (page 122), is a beautiful example of an iron terminal. The crowning figure and fleur-de-lis are gilded, while signs and symbols of the Zodiac are worked around the outer and inner open-framed globes. Simpler vanes are common throughout the country, attached to farmhouses or stables. That from Broek (page 122) is shaped like a swan; one may be seen at Veere which takes the form of a ship. The shaft of the weathercock from Hees (page 124) is made up of iron scrolls, welded together, and four projecting arms point to north, south, east and west.

The leadwork to be observed on domestic buildings is not of remarkable interest. There are no wonderful decorated rain-water heads such as may be

HOORN, NORTH HOLLAND

FRANEKER, FRIESLAND (CURVED GABLES DATED 1573)

HOVDEN SYNG
1612

CARVED STONE LETTERING FROM HAARLEM

seen elsewhere, and lead heads, when used at all, are for the most part comparatively plain, square projections. The examples from Zutphen, reproduced on page 122, illustrate two ordinary forms. An interesting feature, prevalent in North Holland, is the lead finial placed at the apex of a hipped roof. There are many examples in the streets of Hoorn, three of which are shown on page 124. Notice should be taken of the delicate little fretwork heads; the repoussé patterns on the upright sides; and the iron vane which surmounts one of the examples. These objects, although of little practical use, have a decorative value that well justifies their existence. In all these exterior features and details, whether executed in wood or stone, metal or brick, there is especial evidence of the type of mind that was concerned with their production; they pertinently give the key to temperament and character. Such work resulted from deliberate thought and calculation, rather than from imaginative impulse. Sometimes it verged on dulness, yet there is always traceable a certain solid strength and vigour. This is well seen in the stone carvings, here illustrated, whose subjects are often lacking in originality or follow some oft-repeated theme. They are excellently carved, however, and attain interest in consequence. For the individuality of the masons is reflected in the inanimate stone. They gave life to their work and freshness to old subjects. Each man followed his own bent. Some were a little in advance of their time, some behind it, so there are endless variations to patterns that superficially agree. A new turn was given to a scroll here, a different arrangement there; just small things that served to raise work from the conventional and commonplace.

CARVED STONE PANEL FROM FRANEKER

CARVED STONE PANEL
FROM ZUTPHEN (DATED 1615)

CARVED STONE PANEL
FROM SNEEK

CARVED STONE PANEL FROM HAARLEM

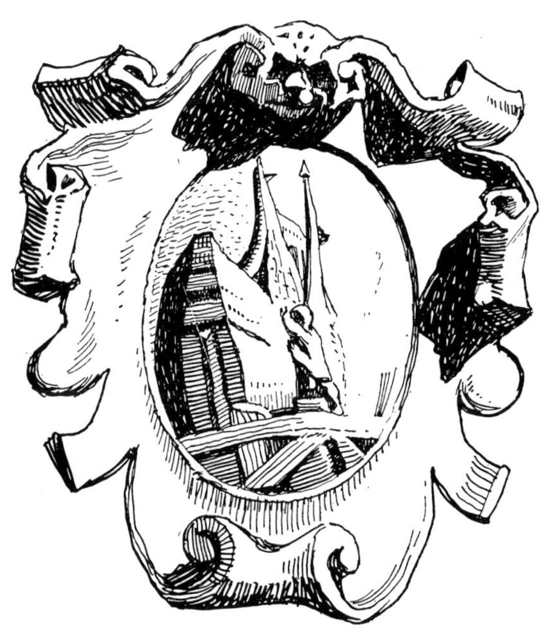

CARVED STONE PANEL
FROM HAARLEM

CARVED STONE PANEL
FROM WORKUM

CARVED STONE PANELS FROM MIDDELBURG, ZEELAND (HOUSE DATED 1590)

The olden craftsmen respected tradition. Forms that became established by custom were handed down from generation to generation. Certain ornaments continued to be used, almost unaltered, over a very long period. Not that patterns were slavishly followed ; on the contrary, each man gave his own interpretation of what he knew had served so well, and fashioned his work in his own way. But he remembered something of that which had gone before. Traditions of ornamentation were just as much founded upon accumulated experience as were the main styles of architecture. The worker saw around him the forces of Nature, active yet unchanging, the abiding waterways, the ancient churches standing as they had done in times long past, and it was in a spirit of respect for the permanence of spiritual and material things that he pursued his craft. This was altogether good. Methods of workmanship, the treatment of features, and types of enrichment, were gradually evolved. They were governed by ordered principles that slowly grew together and became established, principles that served to check the introduction of inharmonious innovations which would have been out of sympathy with all those forms that, as a whole, were customary and usual.

CARVED STONE PANEL FROM HAARLEM

WOUDRICHEM, NORTH BRABANT (DATED 1606 AND 1593)

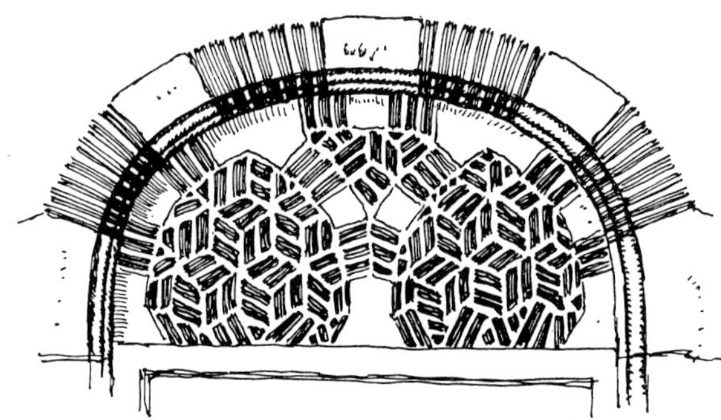

BRICK AND STONE MOSAIC FROM ZWOLLE

BRICK AND STONE MOSAIC FROM NIJMEGEN

The national temperament always asserted itself and each individual as he carved his stone, laid his bricks, worked his wood, or wrought his iron, did his small part to keep alive the inherited traditions, and pass them on so that they should be vigorous to meet the needs of future generations.

The ornamental features that appear on the exterior walls impart to the buildings of Holland much of that quaintness for which they are distinguished. Although the decorations are so plentifully applied, they do not often appear misplaced or offend the eye. For the natural conditions of the country have always been peculiar. The low-lying lands and ever-present water demand a special type of architecture which shall be in thorough sympathy with the surroundings, as well as outwardly express the character of those people who live amongst them. Much is possible and good in Holland which would be out of place, or even bad, elsewhere. The many houses, appearing where they do, are

Doorways, windows, gables and ornaments, therefore, by their particular appearance, mark various steps in a long-continued process of development. Period followed period. After the pointed-arched doorways came the circular-headed ; gables of simple outline in course of time became more complex ; fashions in the shaping of wall-ties changed. But nothing happened suddenly. Craftsmen were content to solve their own problems without any show of haste. It was by such methods that incongruities were avoided.

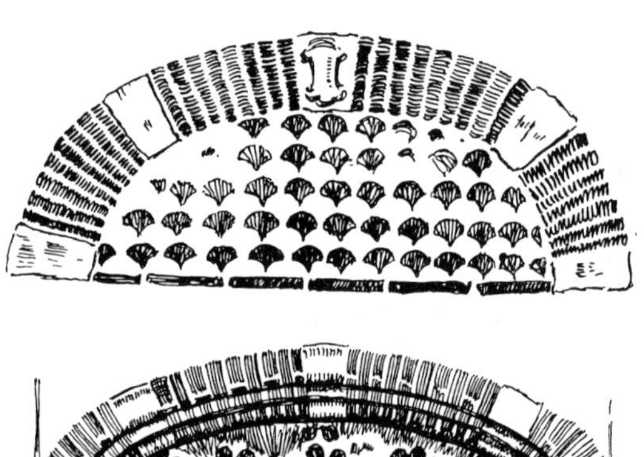

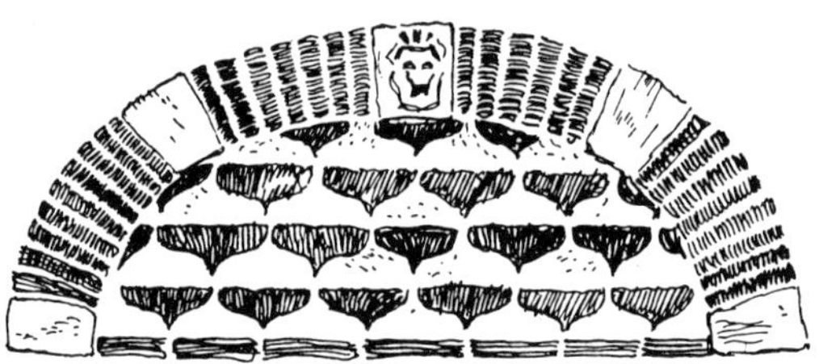

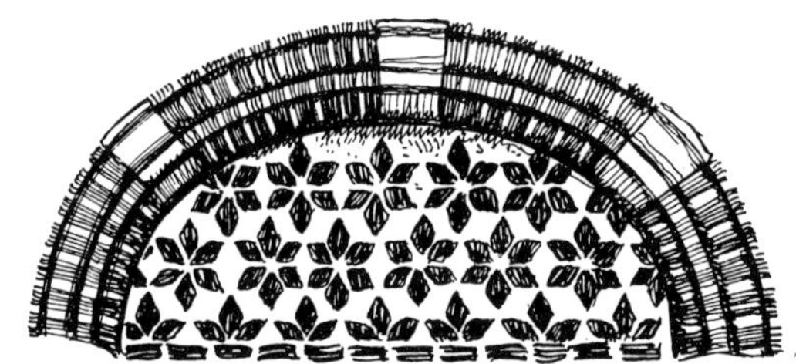

BRICK AND STONE MOSAICS FROM WOUDRICHEM

ZWOLLE, OVERIJSSEL (DATED 1609)

DETAIL OF DIAPER-WORK FROM FRANEKER

admirably conceived. Rich with ornaments, date panels, little carvings, mosaics and ironwork —such as are shown by the illustrations in this section—with coloured bricks fashioned in many ways, and doorways and windows highly decorated, they cannot fail to appeal to those who see them in their natural environment. There is a personal note about each dwelling. They are houses that look like homes, places to be treasured by succeeding generations. And the evidences of pride of possession to be seen in the isolated panels carved with arms, dates and inscriptions, or similar motives worked around doorways, especially give to the brick and stone-built walls a home-like and fireside quality. Students of English architecture will have observed how homely ideas affected the appearance of the houses of Holland just as they did those of England. Similar sentiments obtained in both countries and indirectly brought kindred features to the buildings. It requires but little imagination to people once again the streets and waterways with men and women and children who lived in bygone centuries. Evidences of their lives are on every hand. The stones they lovingly caused to be carved are there; the heavy studded doors that yielded to their hands are still framed by old entrance ways. The work was done that it should last and yet it stands, solid and good. The glory of the house may have departed; yet there still remains the material record of lives well-spent and duties well-performed. And in this the carved monograms and dates are full of meaning.

WORKUM, FRIESLAND

ENAMELLED EARTHENWARE TILES (EARLY 18TH CENTURY)

ENAMELLED EARTHENWARE TILES (EARLY 18TH CENTURY)

IRON WALL-TIES

A N O 1 6 8 5

IRON DATE-SIGN FROM ST. ANNA, NEAR NIJMEGEN

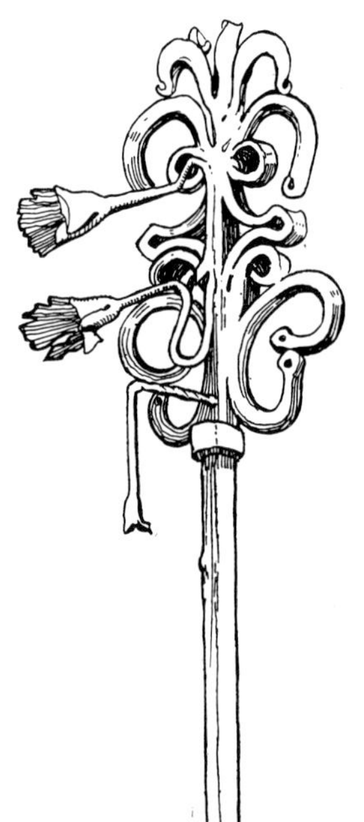

OVAL WINDOW, WITH
STANCHION BAR, FROM LEIDEN

IRON WEATHER-
VANE FROM BROEK

IRON WALL-TIE
FROM NIJMEGEN

LEAD SPOUT-HEAD
FROM ZUTPHEN

IRON TERMINAL
FROM MIDDELBURG

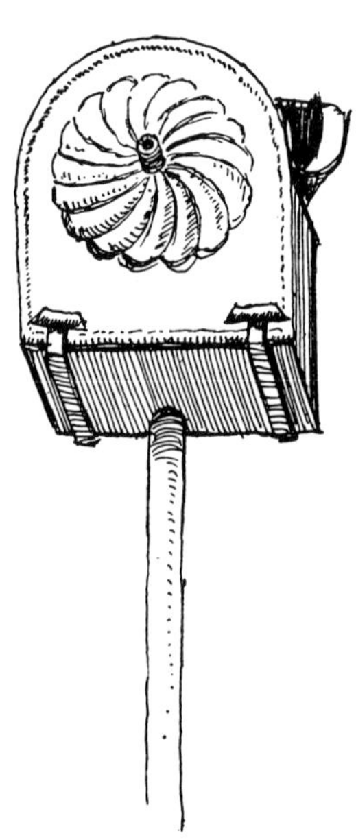

LEAD SPOUT-HEAD
FROM ZUTPHEN

IRON WALL-TIE FROM BEUGEN

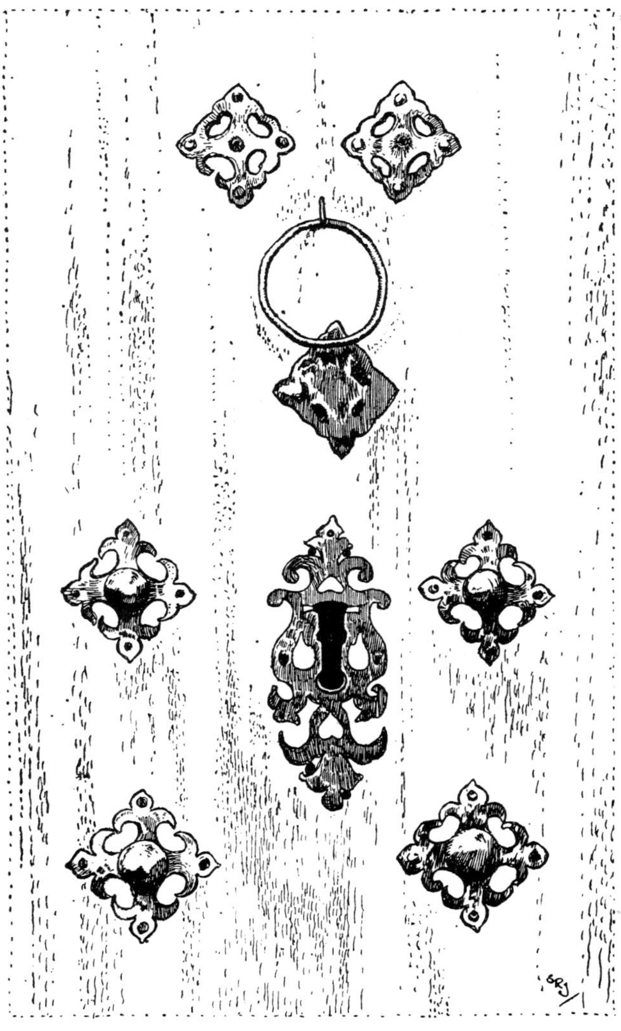

IRON DOOR-FURNITURE FROM MIDDELBURG

IRON DOOR-KNOCKER

IRON WEATHER-VANE FROM HEES

LEAD FINIAL FROM HOORN

LEAD FINIAL FROM HOORN

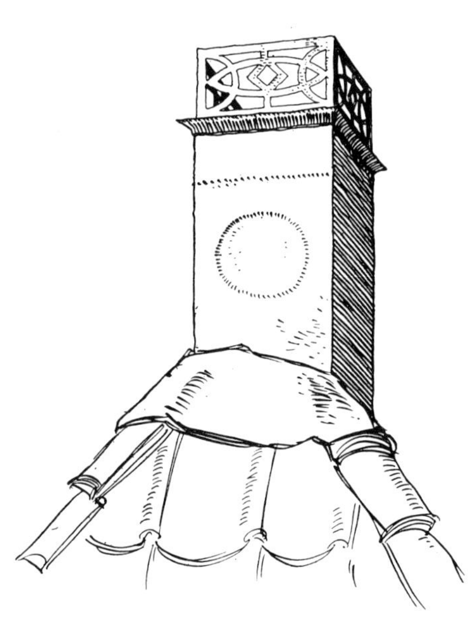

LEAD FINIAL FROM HOORN

DIVISION III

INTERIORS AND DECORATION

III.—INTERIORS AND DECORATION

THERE are, within the old buildings of Holland, interior effects of rare charm. They are hidden away from the outer world behind high gabled fronts of sober houses, beyond the thresholds of country farms. These interiors are rich in memories of the past. They tell of bygone times and bring vivid pictures of civic and home life to the imagination. Solidly built, they were erected with due thought to permanence, that they should stand from generation to generation; that men's memories might be honoured by their children and their children's children. That it should be continuous and abiding was the keynote of the old work which to this day is fresh and beautiful, full of life and vitality, although the makers of it have long since gone and are forgotten. And while things were made to be durable, so also were they made to please the eye and gratify the senses. Good construction, accompanied by much enrichment, gave results tending towards extreme elaboration. Rooms became imposing by their massive ceiling beams supported by sculptured corbels; panelling, or maybe Spanish leather or tapestry, upon the walls; carved oaken doors; fireplaces in wood and stone adorned with columns, figures and other devices; coloured tiles of many patterns; cast-iron firebacks and wrought metalwork; panels of painted glass in the windows; floors of oak, veined marble, or glazed quarries; brass candelabrums hanging from the ceilings, with movable furniture and ornaments disposed in many places.

A good impression of a seventeenth-century room may be gathered from the accompanying illustration from Dordrecht (page 128). The walls are panelled in oak up to a certain height; above is a deep white frieze, admirably adapted for displaying the blue-and-white ware and pictures which rest against it. The chimney-piece is sumptuous, alternately gay and sober, charming below the mantel with brightly-coloured tiles and shining metal utensils, dignified above with panelling and projecting frieze. Forming the dividing line between mantel and fireplace is a mantel-cloth of blue material, inscribed with the homely maxim "Oost West, Thuis

BRASS CANDELABRUM FROM HAARLEM

SEVENTEENTH-CENTURY ROOM FROM DORDRECHT, SOUTH HOLLAND

SEVENTEENTH-CENTURY ROOM FROM LEEUWARDEN, FRIESLAND

Best," and bearing a brace of crossed tobacco-pipes worked at each end of it. A good specimen of a brass candelabrum is attached to the central ceiling beam, while the floor is covered with matting. Solid oak furniture, massive and heavy, completes this picture of material comfort and pleasantness. Equally characteristic is the room at Leeuwarden (page 129). Similar features will be observed—panelling and carved woodwork; ceiling joists and beams, which are here supported by moulded corbels; blue-and-white ware, tiles, and a blue velvet mantel-cloth. The hearth is of squares of black and white marble. Upon it stands a copper fire-holder; behind is a cast-iron fireback adorned with an armorial subject. In the lead-glazed window are two circular panels of painted glass.

Another example of a brass candelabrum, similar to the one above-mentioned, is shown by the drawing from Haarlem (page 127). It is of a type that was customary. Many such still exist in old-world rooms, suspended from high ceilings by chains or rods. Apart from their uses for purposes of illumination, they are highly successful as centre ornaments, for it will be seen how effectively they were made, with curved decorated brackets branching from shaped shafts. Patterns are various, but there are certain essentials common to all and a general resemblance between each. Thus, a particularly beautiful candelabrum in the Town Hall at Zwolle, with an image of the Virgin and pierced, leaf-like brackets, is but an elaboration of the simple familiar form. Some carry three lights only, ordinarily there are ten or twelve; while an example noticed at Haarlem, with twenty-seven candles, probably represents the extreme capacity of this old-fashioned system of lighting.

Of interior features, first in importance come the fireplaces. Great thought was given to the decoration of them, the appearance of many being rich beyond

FIREPLACE IN THE BRICKLAYERS' GUILD, AMSTERDAM (17TH CENTURY)

FIREPLACE FROM MAASTRICHT, LIMBURG (DATED 1510)

CAST-IRON FIREBACK FROM LEIDEN

description. Numerous kinds of materials were used for their adornment; brick and stone, wood, marble and slate, coloured tiles and terra-cotta, all giving value to the imposing compositions. And although the materials were so various, they were skilfully combined to produce harmonious results. Fireplaces were brought forward from the walls and not set back within them. The openings were of ample size, wide and high. The jambs, enriched with mouldings or appearing as columns, supported massive hoods that extended upwards to the ceiling.

The fireplace at Maastricht (page 131) is a good specimen of the late Gothic type. It belongs to the year 1510, this date being carved on the centre scroll. Upon the sandstone jambs are worked Gothic mouldings which spring from shaped stops resting on square bases. The broad frieze is rich with carvings of angels, conventional flowers, cusps, and two shields, bearing the arms of Maastricht and Liège. The rear of the opening is lined with pressed terra-cotta tiles that exhibit a variety of designs in low relief. Against it is set an iron fireback ornamented with a heraldic device. The wooden figures on the mantel-shelf are merely placed thereon and are not inherent to the design.

Details of fireplaces changed with the passing of Gothic influences, although the olden form was still retained. Classic columns, or less frequently, human figures and grotesques, were substituted for moulded jambs. They commonly supported a carved oak frieze surmounted by a projecting cornice. Such chimney-pieces are by no means rare in Holland and may generally be ascribed to the seven-

CAST-IRON FIREBACK FROM NIJMEGEN

FIREPLACE FROM MIDDELBURG, ZEELAND

CAST-IRON FIREBACK
FROM MIDDELBURG

teenth century. One, from Leeuwarden, has already been illustrated on page 129. Another example, from Middelburg, is here given (page 133). The columns are of white marble, but the jambs behind them, together with the bases and corbels, are of slate and are decorated with strapwork patterns. The oak mantel is inlaid with bands and panels of light wood. Tiles of blue, white and yellow cover the back, and border the upright sides of the iron hearth.

The chimney-piece at Amsterdam (page 130) is of an unusual pattern. It is situated in the room of the Bricklayers' Guild and is of early seventeenth-century workmanship. The opening is framed of stone. Over the mantel-shelf is a curved pediment with the arms of Amsterdam carved upon it. Fitted to the chimney-breast above is a small oval painted panel enclosed by brickwork.

The fireplace from the Westerwold (page 135), now at Groningen, belongs to a later period than the preceding example. A wooden chimney-shelf and pilasters, almost black in colour, support the tapering hood. The back of the fireplace is faced with blue-and-white tiles and red bricks. A protecting fireback rests against it, while a hanger, hooked within the opening, holds the metal pot over the fire. The effect of this fireplace and its accessories, admirably decorative in themselves, is further enhanced by the pure white surrounding walls, and by the parti-coloured floor laid with red and yellow quarries.

Cast-iron firebacks have been noticed in the previous illustrations. They were generally used where fires burned on open hearths. The

CAST-IRON FIREBACK FROM JISP

FIREPLACE FROM THE WESTERWOLD, GRONINGEN

INTERIOR OF A WOODEN HOUSE AT MARKEN, NORTH HOLLAND

castings are rather light and thin, and were taken from wooden models. They are ornamented with floral and heraldic subjects, or designs suggested by classical myths and bible stories. Of the four examples illustrated on pages 132 and 134, two have armorial bearings, surrounded by rich borders, cast upon them. The one from Leiden is dated 1609, and the other, from Nijmegen, 1650. Both the remaining specimens, from Jisp and Middelburg, are decorated with figure subjects, bordered by fruit and scrolls and flowers. All the work is in rather low relief.

Fuel, in the form of peat or charcoal, was responsible for certain utensils in which it could be conveniently burned. One such is given on page 139. It is an iron fire-standard suited for holding peat, and was drawn in the Museum at Dordrecht. The lines of the design are good, especially to be observed in the engaged scrolls and shaping of the top. It is, withal, serviceably made. Small boxes containing fire, placed upon the floor in front of chairs, served as foot-warmers (page 148). They are of square or oval

BRASS CHIMNEY-CRANE FROM LEEUWARDEN

DELFT DISHES (18TH CENTURY)

DELFT DISHES (18TH CENTURY)

HINDELOOPEN ROOM AT THE FRISIAN MUSEUM, LEEUWARDEN

shape. The sides are frequently patterned and the lids perforated. Fires were also contained in iron pots which stood upon oak stools within the fireplaces; or they burned in little iron hearths, which were set towards the centre of the rooms, with no provision made for carrying away the smoke. The former system is exemplified by the drawing from Leeuwarden (page 137), and the latter by an illustration from a cottage at Marken (page 136).

A small crane is often seen attached to the back of the fireplace. A kettle or pot rests upon it, which might, if desired, be swung over or away from the fire. The specimen here reproduced (page 136) is from Leeuwarden. It has one simple movement, that of swinging backwards and forwards. The curved arm is made of brass, and shaped to resemble a fish. Out of the mouth comes the iron kettle-holder with a small chain affixed, handy for drawing it to and fro. Allied to the crane, and used for a similar purpose, is the hanger that was suspended from the flue. The two specimens appearing on page 139 are from Middelburg, and both are constructed of iron. They can be made to hang high or low, one by means of a ratchet, and the other by a catch, which fits into pierced holes and is shown in detail.

The set of fire-irons, also from Middelburg (page 139), furnishes admirable examples of useful objects, suitably adorned. The plate to which the fire-irons hang, with scallop-like indentations at its upper edge, is enriched with incised decoration, depicting a ship, trees, birds, letters, and the date of 1787. The tongs at the extreme left are so fashioned that one arm, being hollow, may be used as a blowpipe. Next in order is a ladle adapted for scooping up ashes from the hearth. Upon the flat handle is further incised ornamentation, based upon floral motives. The central object is a blowpipe, and a second pair of tongs completes the set. With the exception of some of the ends and terminations, which are of brass, these implements are made of iron, brightly polished.

In the glazed tiles, inseparably associated with Delft and other places in Holland, the Dutch had admirable material for interior decoration. Some tiles were pure white; others had conventional floral forms painted upon them. Many, again, were decorated with devices derived from scriptural, nautical, rural, historical, and classical sources. Units such

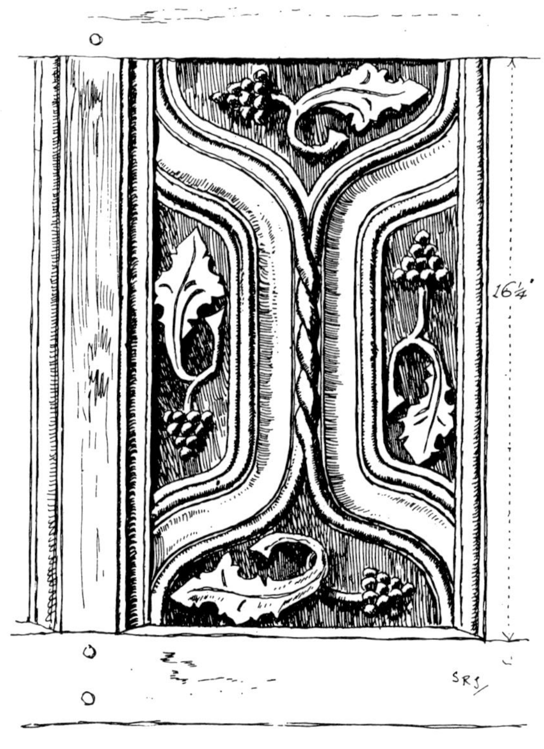

CARVED OAK PANEL FROM ZWOLLE (16TH CENTURY)

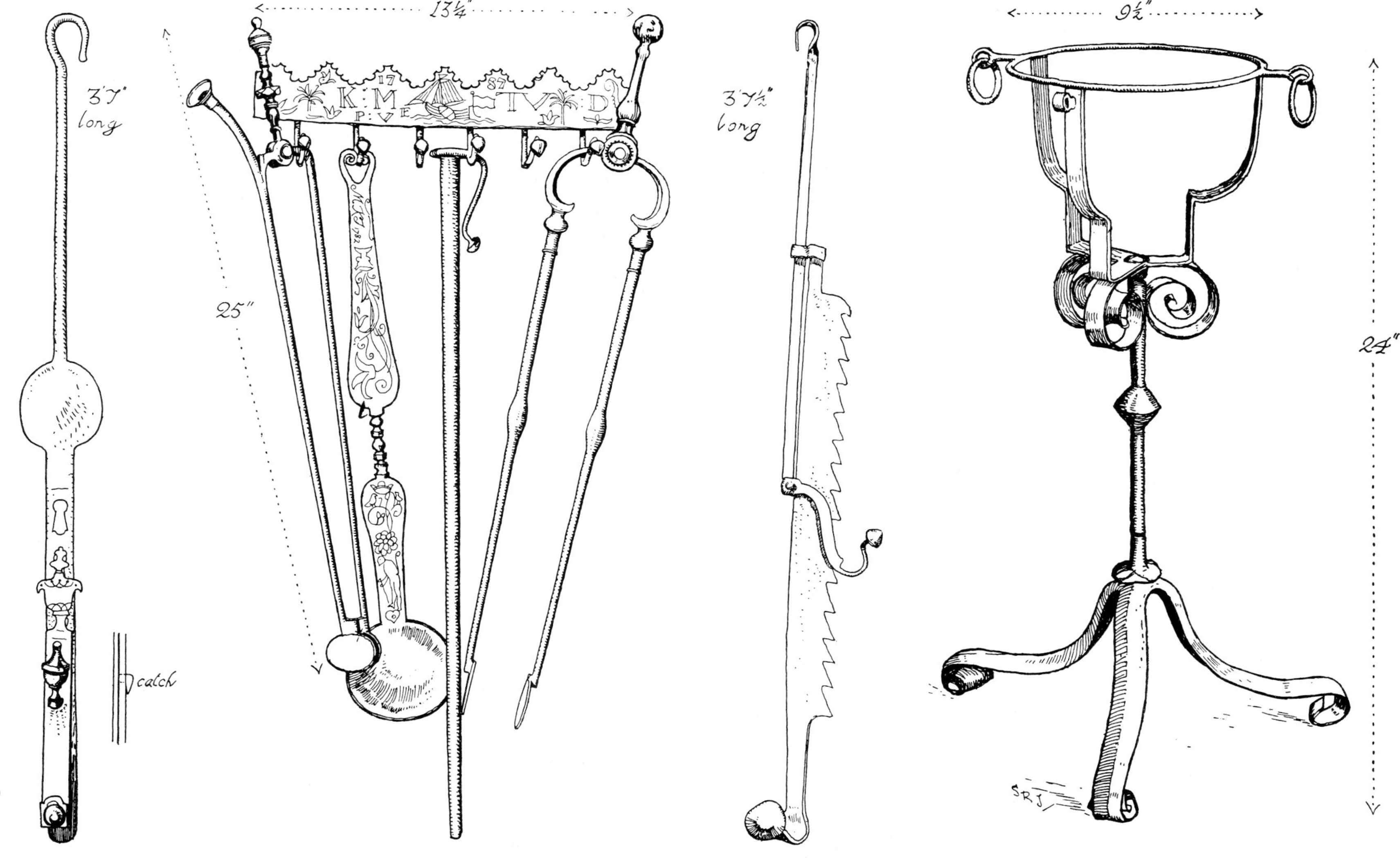

IRON HANGERS, FIRE-IRONS AND FIRE-STANDARD

as these, beautiful in themselves, were capable of giving lively and gay effects when arranged together. How satisfactorily they were used will have been already observed in the fireplaces previously described.

But, apart from giving value to fireplaces, they were employed in other ways. Notable rooms are to be seen whose good appearance depends primarily upon the skilful manipulation of tiles. Two such are illustrated, one in colour (opposite). They are from Hindeloopen, and are now in the Frisian Museum at Leeuwarden. The original woodwork of the coloured drawing belongs to the seventeenth century. The back of the fireplace, as well as the walls surrounding it, is faced entirely with tiles from floor to ceiling. Those towards the floor have blue and white patterns upon them; above, and in the window recess, they are white but for the narrow blue borders round the angles. These tiles were made at Makkum. Upon the floor are glazed quarries of red and black, laid in alternate colours. The room of the other illustration (page 137) dates from the eighteenth century. It has similar tiles on the walls and quarries on the floor. Floors were also laid with other coloured quarries, blue and green and yellow; while in larger houses stone and marble were employed with pleasing results.

Panelling was by no means infrequently applied to interior walls. It was often marked by elaboration rather than simplicity, although there are not wanting examples of rooms wainscoted with plain framed woodwork divided into panels by stiles and rails. Of ornamental panels there are certain definite kinds. Characteristic are those adorned with linen-fold patterns. Another design that was favoured is shown in the illustration taken from Zwolle (page 138), where carved vine ornaments appear between two curved and moulded scrolls set back to back. This particular example is attributed to the beginning of the sixteenth century. At a later date round-headed arches and pilasters were introduced, such as those exemplified from Leiden on this page, as well as carved friezes and moulded cornices. It is remarkable to note the great similarity between the development of panelling in Holland and in England. The earlier patterns employed in both countries are practically identical, while Dutch

OAK PANELLING FROM LEIDEN

HINDELOOPEN ROOM AT THE FRISIAN MUSEUM, LEEUWARDEN

seventeenth-century woodwork bears great resemblance to that of our Jacobean period.

Wooden doors harmonised with the wainscot of the walls. They were divided into panels and often richly carved. Doorways were given importance by the pilasters and cornices that surrounded them. The door from Groningen (below) furnishes a seventeenth-century specimen, elaborately carved with forms peculiar to the time.

The metal fittings attached to doors—locks, bolts, hinges, handles, and the like—are of good design and workmanship. Two lock-plates (page 143), from the Rijks Museum at Amsterdam, belong to the sixteenth century. They are both made of iron. One, bearing the date of 1587, is decorated with projecting ornaments; the other is adorned with applied metalwork, pierced and carved. Further examples of iron door-furniture, simply but effectively treated, are illustrated by the handle from Middelburg and the bolt from Dordrecht (page 143).

A feature common to Dutch rooms is the small cupboard in the wall, wherein many and sundry articles were stored. The recess is sometimes merely covered by a curtain that may be drawn to and fro, such as can be seen at the left hand of the window in the coloured reproduction from Leeuwarden given here. But generally a wooden door was fitted to the opening. Some of these doors, with one or two panels, are quite plainly made. Others, highly decorated with carvings and metalwork, furnish examples of beautiful craftsmanship. Two are here illustrated (pages 143 and 144), which show how well and cunningly artificers in wood and metal exercised their skill. Both are of sixteenth-century workmanship, and are now in the Rijks Museum. Apart from the good wood-carving, the ironwork on each is notable. The three hinges, attached to the larger door, all have peculiarly graceful branched

CARVED DOOR FROM GRONINGEN (17TH CENTURY)

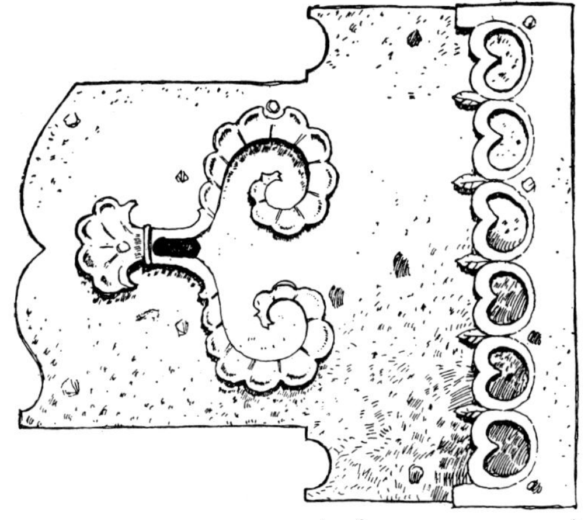

IRON LOCK-PLATE (16TH CENTURY)

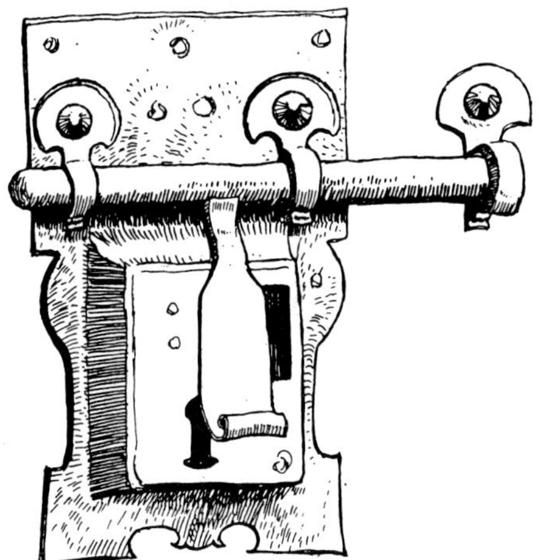

IRON LOCK AND BOLT

CARVED DOOR OF WALL-CUPBOARD, WITH PIERCED AND ENGRAVED IRON FITTINGS

IRON LOCK-PLATE
(DATED 1587)

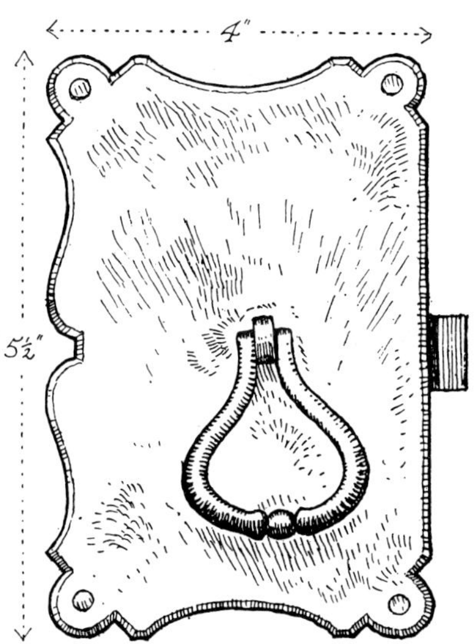

IRON DOOR-HANDLE AND ESCUTCHEON

terminations; while the hinge of the second example is pierced and engraved with a floral pattern. The lock-plates, also, are admirably devised. The further illustration of a Hindeloopen room from Leeuwarden (page 141) is especially interesting, for around the walls are cupboard-like apartments that afforded accommodation for sleeping. They are closed by wooden doors which have open-work panels at their heads to permit the passage of air. The beds, resembling a ship's berths, are reached by flights of steps, two of which will be seen in the reproduction. These steps are movable and curiously shaped and painted, as is demonstrated by the flight in the foreground with its side boards made to imitate birds and flowers. Other old Dutch interiors—cheerful with coloured plates, tiles and quarries, shining brass and carved woodwork—furnish instances of this particular disposition of sleeping accommodation.

The old furniture was of a kind that well harmonised with the fitted woodwork and other decorations of the rooms. It is not unusual to find pieces of the seventeenth and eighteenth centuries amid surroundings similar to those for which they were originally intended. The rooms at Dordrecht (page 128) and Groningen (page 135) both have suitable furniture that valuably contributes to the success of the schemes. All is more or less directly useful ; rooms were not crowded with objects that were neither utilitarian nor good to look upon. Most commonly occurring are chairs and tables, chests and cabinets. The earlier oak work was jointed and pegged together. It was very solidly made and ornamented in a reasonable way. Some of the large cabinets offer splendid examples of skilful handiwork, and an elaborate specimen, from Haarlem, appears on page 145. Two characteristic tables are also illustrated, one from Edam (page 145) and one from Amsterdam (page 146). In the eighteenth century it became the fashion in certain parts of Holland to heavily paint fitted and movable furniture with coloured patterns, the natural

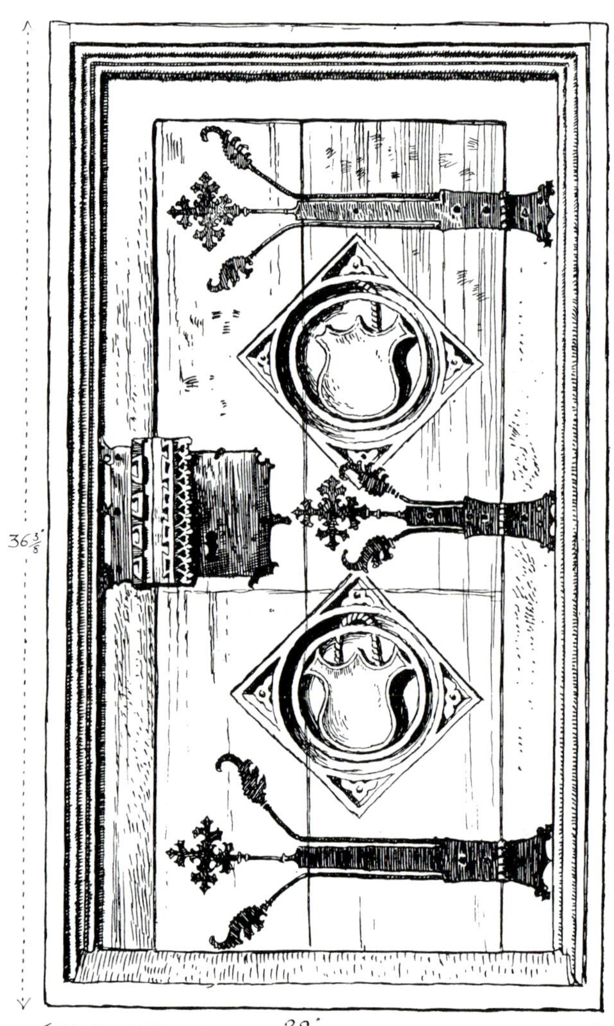

WALL-CUPBOARD WITH IRON LOCK AND HINGES (16TH CENTURY)

beauty of the wood being thus obscured. All kinds of objects were ornamented, and in a somewhat amateurish way. The favoured motifs were floral scrolls, little flowers, birds and animals, scriptural scenes, with pastoral and sea views.

CARVED TABLE FROM EDAM

Brass was much used in the making of domestic utensils. Familiar objects for many purposes were fashioned of this material. Brightly polished and shining, they were quite in accord with the prevailing gayness of the rooms and well harmonised with the fitted woodwork, furniture, tiles and other metalwork. Fireplaces were adorned with sundry articles of brass, some being purely ornamental, others achieving some useful mission. The brass chimney-crane (page 136) belongs to this latter class, as does the fire-side set reproduced on page 147. The latter is a particularly handy contrivance, for, being movable, it can be transferred from room to room. The stand takes the form of a baluster stem which rests upon an ornamental basic tripod; it is surmounted by a circular attachment that supports the kettle. Upon three curved arms, branching outwardly, the brush and tongs and shovel are hooked. This set is of eighteenth-century workmanship. The stand is 1 foot 11½ inches high, the tongs 23 inches long, the brush 21 inches long, and the shovel 23 inches long. An example of the portable foot-warmers for placing on the floor in front of chairs, such as have been already mentioned, is here illustrated (page 148). It is made of brass and has eight sides. Each upright side is decorated with repoussé

CARVED CABINET FROM HAARLEM

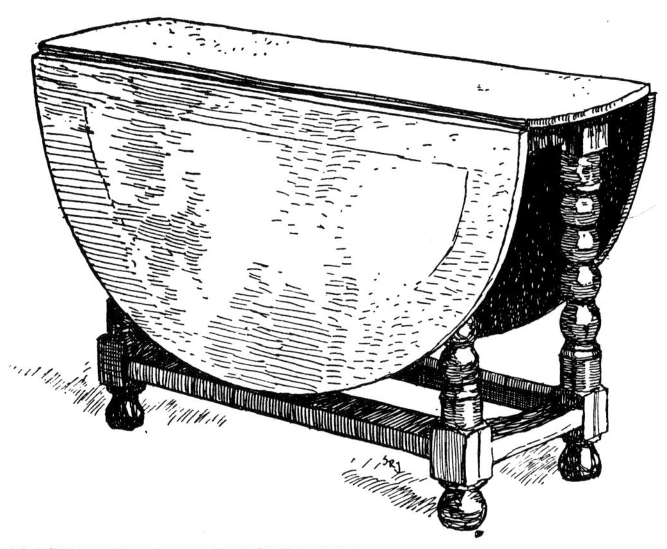

TABLE FROM AMSTERDAM

work, circular bosses alternating with panels of flowers. The slightly curved top has a medallion in the centre, engraved with the letters and date "I. W. HM. 1733." It is surrounded with floral scrolls, geometrically arranged, and between the patterns are pierced holes through which the heat is distributed.

The candlestick (page 148), also of brass, belongs to the eighteenth century. It has two curved brackets which are adjustable, as will be seen by the hinged attachments in the illustration. The height is 18¼ inches and the width, from bracket to bracket, is 12⅛ inches. Another old-fashioned object used for lighting is the brass lantern with arched top (page 148). All the three windows are surrounded by a border of floral openwork, very finely pierced with a pattern common to the eighteenth century. The fourth side, forming the back, has a panel in the centre.

The cover of the warming-pan, given on page 147, furnishes an excellent specimen of perforated and engraved brasswork. The central figures represent Venus and Cupid, while interwoven with the strap and foliated ornaments are grotesque figures, beasts and birds. Each little part of the design is engraved, and around the outer margin of the pan is a Dutch inscription which embodies the date of 1602. Further well-executed piercing and engraving, but of a later date than the above, appear on the tea-caddy here illustrated (page 148). This latter object is 6 inches high and 4 inches wide. The pastille-burner (page 148) is made wholly of brass. Upon the baluster

WROUGHT-IRON STAIR-RAILING FROM ZIERIKZEE

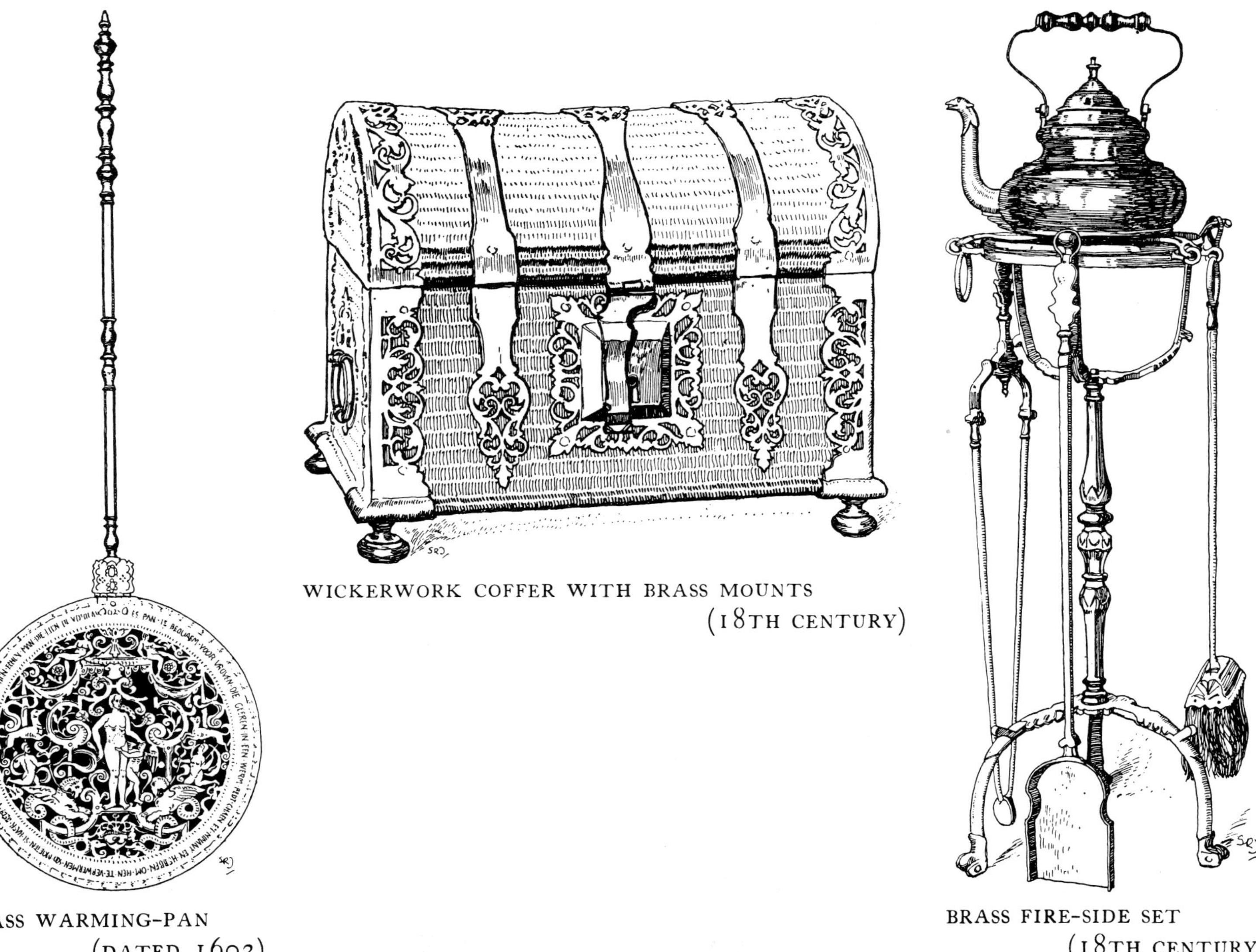

BRASS WARMING-PAN
(DATED 1602)

WICKERWORK COFFER WITH BRASS MOUNTS
(18TH CENTURY)

BRASS FIRE-SIDE SET
(18TH CENTURY)

BRASS CANDLESTICK (18TH CENTURY)

BRASS TEA-CADDY (18TH CENTURY)

BRASS PASTILLE-BURNER

BRASS FOOT-WARMER (DATED 1733)

BRASS LANTERN (18TH CENTURY)

CORRIDOR IN "ST. PIETERSHOFJE," HOORN, NORTH HOLLAND

TILED FIREPLACE FROM VOLENDAM, NORTH HOLLAND

stem and circular base are rococo designs beaten-up in relief. Made of wickerwork, the coffer reproduced cn page 147 is adorned with handsomely shaped and perforated brass mounts that extend around it.

The corridor at Hoorn (page 149) belongs to the seventeenth century. It has a timber roof springing from the two side-walls in the form of a barrel-vault. Upon the concave surface are longitudinal and transverse ribs whose intersections are emphasised by carved bosses. The vault is supported at each side by decorated wooden brackets. Another detail associated with a place of access is the wrought-iron railing from Zierikzee (page 146).

And lastly, three typical village interiors are given. Two, from Volendam (above) and Marken (page 151), have simple fireplaces faced with ordinary blue and white Dutch tiles. Another shows a room in a wooden house at Marken (page 152), the timbering of the walls being visible.

But it is the old towns of Holland, rather than the villages, that hold the charms for those who sojourn in that fascinating country; towns rich in associations that unbrokenly date back to a buried and untraceable antiquity. In them history has been made. There stand the old and sober gabled buildings, silent monuments to the thoughts, ideals and ambitions of those who built them. And, clustering around the market-places where life yet centres as it did in days gone by, or reflected in still waters, the houses keep their secrets well.

Sydney R. Jones.

TILED FIREPLACE FROM MARKEN, NORTH HOLLAND

INTERIOR OF A WOODEN HOUSE AT MARKEN, NORTH HOLLAND